AUTONOMY

Edited by Vilmos Ágoston
Translated by Éva Lengyel, Iván Sellei and
Gábor Rózsa

MATTHIAS CORVINUS PUBLISHING CO.

BUFFALO-TORONTO

Lectures held at the Conference on Autonomy,
November 18-20, 1993,
organized by the Hungarian Alliance of Free Democrats,
the Dutch Liberal Party, D66 and the
German Friedrich Naumann Foundation.

The original bilingual edition was supported by the:
Friedrich Nauman Foundation

First English Edition

ISBN 1-882785-07-X

Library of Congress Catalogue Card Number:
95-75131

Cover by Márta Regényi

Autonomy:

Preface to the   North American   Edition

In American and Canadian politics the very concept of "group" or "national" autonomy is unfamiliar, nay even alien. With this in mind, I think it is important to say a little about the concept so that semantic confusion does not lead to out of hand rejection of a dialogue on this subject.

In the American and Canadian context autonomy is used primarily to describe the defenses that individuals have within society or against government encroachment on their personal existence. In this usage the terms applies basically to "personal space", to matters of privacy, to concerns of the individual for protection against unjustifiable social intrusion into what belongs to the personal lives of people. In these societies the concept is rarely used to designate group or collective rights.

On the continent of Europe autonomy was widely accepted in relation to certain kinds of institutions, particularly churches and universities. In the Middle Ages, feudalism as a socio-economic <u>and</u> political order, also provided decentralisation of authority, which meant that there existed a great deal of territorial, regional, and local autonomy in day-to-day decision-making.

For example the pre-Mohacs (1526) Kingdom of Hungary this meant administrative decentralization which allowed Croatia and Transylvania significant self-government for hundreds of years, and extensive self-government for Saxon and Szekely settlements. Within the context of the Ottoman Turkish empire autonomy i.e., self-government was also guaranteed to the different non-Islamic religious communities or "millets". That is, their respective church leaders, while

1

they could not exercise authority over territory, they could do so over their own believers in community legal matters as well as doctrinal concerns.

Unfortunately, the French Revolution destroyed not only the authoritarian legacy of the past, but also European commitments to decentralisation and institutional pluralism. Popular sovereignty replaced monarchy and divine rule of kings, but it also brought with it a majoritarians intolerance that undermined many long-established rights and oppurtinities for local self-government and interest representation.

Fortunately the United States and Canada inherited political traditions that did not follow majoritarian intolerance and centralisation as guiding principles. In both of these states, the size of their territories, the diversity of their religious and ethnic subgrups required the istitutionalization of decentralization. This meant that in both cases federalism guaranteed respect and maintenance of regional and traditional differences. In both these states it was economic development, industrialization and urbanization that produced integration, rather than assimilationist cultural policies driven by shauvinistic nationalisms.

The American and Canadian experiences also differed in one other respect from the European Continent. Aside from the reservations set aside for the conquered native Americans, the legal status of inhabitants were "never" linked to group rights. The never is in quotation marks because of the significant exception of Quebec. In relation to the latter Canadian province, the federalism of Canada has protected group rights with the guarantee of "territorial autonomy". Altough this not the name it goes by, this is what it boils down to.

For the rest of North America, excepting only Mexico where the <u>fueros</u> of colonial times did leave some group rights intact,

2

individual rights became the norm. But because these individual rights also guaranteed the rights to economic, social, cultural, and political association and organization, this meant that groups could sustain their own schools (parochial or private), cultural clubs, churches and other significant "private" institutions.

In East-Central Europe in the 20th century, the French model of the centralized unitary nation-state and majoritarian democracy, combined with the vengeful aftermath of two world wars, and the institutionalization of Communist "democratic centralism", make it well nigh impossible for minorities to defend themselves against the homogenizing tyranny of the majority Staatsvolk nationalities.

An interesting twist to all this is the confusion of the concept of autonomy with the Soviet and Yugoslav attempts to overcome the nationally, ethnically and religiously fragmented conditions prevailing within their borders. Unfortunately, the use of autonomy by these now failed state-systems, makes autonomy suspect in the eyes of Western observers in the region.

However, these same observers forget to consider that the system worked while a modicum of tolerance and compromise prevailed. The system collapsed because of the emergence of exclusivist nationalist demands. In Romania it was the Communist leader Nicolae Ceausescu that led the nationalist frenzy against the Hungarian Bolyai University and the Hungarian Autonomous Region of Eastern Transylvania (even when it was only symbolic autonomy). In Yugoslavia it was the Communist Serb Slobodan Milosevic who led the charge against the Autonomous Province of Kosovo (Albanians) and the Autonomous Province of Vojvodina (Hungarians and others). It may now be seen from these examples that political leaders who had gotten used to a monopoly of power now use the nationalisms of majorities to undergird their control. The mixture of Communist democratic centralism, French unitary statism and the veneer of majoritarian democracy can only lead to Bosnia-like solutions. It is in the light of these grave prospects that the major powers and Western Statesmen must take a serious second look at the institutialization of group rights and structural arangements like autonomy. if genocide and ethocide are to be prevented, the a viable legal and institutional framework must be adopted for the defense of minority rights.

Within the American setting, and the larger Anglo-Saxon legal word, the main defense of group rights and distinct community interest, has been achieved via strong constitutional and contractual traditions and garaantees. From the writings of the contract theorists, particularly John Locke, through the constitutional practices during the formative years of the early Republic to the legalese of present-day corporation lawyers: contracts, charters and constitutions, grant rights and define obligations in society. Implicit in all of this is the right to organize, the right to join groups that we can identify with in terms of our interests: economic, religious, cultural or political. From the Mayflower Compact to the latest variations on debates about "state rights" or "affirmative action" there looms the commitment to a "government of laws and not of men", a society in which both the public and the private, and the relationship between them, is defined by contract.

In the U.S.A. and Canada the concept of contract is ingrained in the political culture and enbedded in legal evolution. Unfortunately in East-Central Europe this tradition has been undermined by the legacies of the French Revolution, and the centralism championed by both the Fascism of the Right and the Left. Szalasi and Rakosi Antonescu and Ceausescu, Tiso and Husak are all part of this destructive legacy. For this reason, in the present context, within the last decade of the 20th century, as regimes, governments, states and nations come to a new sense of their roles within historic evolution, the most important lesson must be the entrenchment of law by contract, governments that become the defenders of rights rather than mechanisms of oppression and exploitation.

Minority rights mean civil and cultural rights. Where popular sovereignty is not yet restrained by constitutionalism and cultural acceptance of the formula majority rule with minority rights, it becomes imperative that minorities acquire specific protections via bilateral, multilateral treaty guarantees and specific "civil rights" legistlation that levels the playing field. Specific contract guarantees of cultural, territorial or personal autonomy may be the only way in which minorities might get to play on such a level field in East-Central Europe.

Andrew Ludanyi
Ohio Northern University

Preface

" A State which is incompetent to satisfy different races condemns itself; a state which labours to neutralize, to absorb, or to expell them, destroys its own vitality; a state which does not include them is destitute of the chief basis of selfgovernment. The theory of nationality, therefore is a retrograde step in history."

(Lord Acton: Nationality, 1862)

The quotation mentioned above by one of the classics of Anglo-Saxon Liberal traditions proves that this prominent representative of Liberalism was well aware of the daunting consequences of unsolved national and minority questions as early as the middle of the nineteenth century. His readers today might find it contradictory that Lord Acton had a realistic knowledge of the existing problems facing mankind and at the same time had an unrealistic expectation of the steady growth of welfare and happiness.

Today we have more sober experience and fewer high-minded illusions. Which of us would dare to claim though that we are in a lot better position than our ancestors? European Liberals at the twilight of the millennium have to face again the challenges of aggressive nationalism and unsolved minority issues. Naturally, history does not repeat itself: the differences are more important than the seemingly ostensible similarities. Nowadays the approach of the Liberals, may they be thinkers, experts or politicians involves less idealism and more practicality.

They do not expect saving solutions from a mysterious invisible hand or from the self-accomplishing ideas of history. On the contrary, they do not believe in any single salutary solution. They hope for tangible results from persistent and purposeful efforts made on the stage of science and politics to achieve more useful and operative solutions. None of them believe in finding a single path towards truth.

There are several alternative and competitive attempts in the developed countries of Europe to solve this problem. These attempts are very difficult to compare and even more difficult to evaluate and rank. Just as minority communities are very different in size, economic and social status, geographical features and in various other characteristics, the same differences exist between these alternative solutions in their details. There is no single, unified model to solve this problem in a general way. Nevertheless, all these more or less acceptable models have something in common: all the minority groups think these solutions are more able to meet their demands and are more beneficial for the given communities than those in any earlier stages.

In the East-Central European countries there are many more promising plans and proposals than real, working solutions. We are behind the developed West in this respect just as much as in other fields of economic and social life.

The conference organized by the Hungarian Alliance of Free Democrats, the Dutch D66 and the German Friedrich Neumann Foundation had a dual purpose:

- to take all the different minority rights in the region into account and examine and map them in a historical perspective and to try and make

a conclusive list of the problems as far as possible and

- to examine all the proposals aimed at assuring minority rights.

Since none of the organizers or participants

expected any salutary solutions from the conference, we can be satisfied with the results. We had so many interesting and useful lectures and debates at the conference that we might well claim they can be useful for a larger public. I am fully convinced they have a message for everybody. Thus, I strongly recommend the book to everybody, may they be Liberals or their rivals, members and supporters of the government, those of the opposition or people who belong to a majority or a minority community. No book could find a larger audience.

István Szent-Iványi
Member of Parliament

Chances of Democracy in the East-Central European Region, A Movement towards Autonomy
Erika Torzsok

> Although the possibilities of choosing
> political activities are quite limited,
> they are unpredictable at the same time

Gabriel A. Almond

I trust it does not sound cynical to use the above quotation as a motto of this essay. We have good reason to think that here and now, in this region, we have a chance to illustrate the truth of this motto quite successfully. That is, although the possibilities of choosing political activities are limited, they are unpredictable at the same time. The postulate I used as a starting point of my reasoning here was that neither the East-Central European countries involved, nor the so-called West was prepared for the breakup of the Soviet Union and the essential political changes after 1989 and neither side had any viable programme.

After 1989, when new political regimes formed and took over power in the region, many people held the belief that all the socio-economic and minority problems of these countries could be solved spontaneously and overnight.

On the contrary, during the past few years it has become very evident that people living in this region are to face an enormously great number of unexpected and unpredictable problems and conflicts. The idea of a united Europe, the unification of the East ant the West cannot be realized in the

9

twinkle of an eye; It is a difficult and long process which requires a lot of effort from both sides. We are bound and determined not only by the present events but also by our remote past. And that is the real core of the problem: which tendency of the European heritage will become stronger and more determining in this region?

Klauss Mann writes about Europe: "Europe has to live with a double postulate to avoid its fall: it has to maintain the awareness of unity, it has to strengthen and deepen the consciousness that Europe is an inseparable unity and, at the same time, it has to keep its variety of styles and traditions alive. Europe means such a precious, but intricate and complicated harmony in which voices of discordance meet in such a way that they do not neutralize each other or themselves."

The question is: what can the political realities of our time achieve with these ideas?

Some say we have arrived close to the end of the last period of the great religious wars and we only have to hold out till the exhaustion of aggression and that we can see some signs pointing us in the direction of a real solution.

One thing seems to be sure: as usual in this region, easy and sweet transition cannot be expected again. We have to face the truth that the fall of communism itself cannot result automatically in the emergence of democratic societies. The interchange between the social structure and the political regime of a given country has to be considered evident and "normal" even in this transitional period of time. Without analysing the recent events in the ex-socialist countries, their economic situation or their social structure I refer the reader to two basic facts:

- After 1989 nationalist tendencies have become stronger

- After 1989 different minorities' struggles for autonomy have strengthened in the region

In the forthcoming passages I would like to confine myself to concentrating on the following problems:

I

a) Why has the endeavour and demand for autonomy become stronger in the post-socialist countries after 1989, and

b) why has this tendency become a suspicious challenge for both some new elite political groups and for the West as such, including some international organizations?

My starting point is as follows: The destabilization of the region is the result of the process of negative modernization taking place in most of the countries involved during the past forty years and not of the efforts or steps taken by minorities. This process involves delayed achievement of a bourgeois type of society, inadequate responses to the challenges of modern times, maintenance of the old, inefficient and unbalanced economic structures, including energy consuming industries, poverty that also includes wasteful spending, financial instability (debts inside and outside the countries), inflation, underdevelopment of the financial systems and practically no reserves. They typically have a very small layer of intellectuals with convertible knowledge, a lack of real commodity production, and a very restricted and out of date structure and range of choice. The level of the economic culture in these countries is very low, their market economy is extremely vulnerable and noncompetitive compared to the West.

Resulting from the facts mentioned above, peoples with various cultural backgrounds suffered from different kinds of

11

problems within the given countries, which represent different models of frustration. Based on these statements I maintain that the minority issue is only "a flower on the hat," not the hat itself. I do not mean to diminish the importance of the question, I only refuse to deal with this problem on purely an emotional level and I would not like to see the dimensions of this question put into a falsely distorted perspective and I am against changing the logical relationship between cause and effect. I must stress, I truly believe, that only democratic changes and tendencies toward liberalization in the economic and social lives of these societies can lead to the resolution of the minority issue, and only the explicit manifestation of the principles of democratic legitimacy and autonomy as political demands can give a real framework for the solution of the minority issue. Therefore, I think it is very harmful to consider the minority question as an issue of utmost importance and give priority to it over everything. It is equally dangerous, of course, if we play down or refuse the importance of the question, since we might misjudge the existing social, economic and cultural tensions and this approach cannot take us any closer to the real solutions either. Minority issue as a tension enhancing factor does not help solve these problems in any way, it only delays the possibility of realizing the actual questions and the proper answers to the real challenges.

These conclusions can be supported by the lessons drawn from most of the previous events in this century. During the past forty years the national interests of every single nation in this region have suffered some injustice in a way and as we know, the foregoing events were determining in this respect as well. István Bibó writes in his work entitled **The Misery of Small States in Eastern Europe:**

"The most serious consequences of the confusion in the territorial status and the distortion of the political culture in the East-Central European countries were the tumult and the distortion of the relationship between the nations living in this region. An outsider, an unattached observer might say that the political life of this region is full of petty and inextricable territorial conflicts and every single nation is in constant discord with practically all of its neighbours."

These statements seem to be just as true in our days as well, even if this struggle ceases for a while from time to time. Since the basic conflicts are unsettled, wars are breaking out again and again in this region.

After the First World War there emerged a real chance to solve these difficulties, that is, according to the principle of peoples' right for self-determination. Bibó writes the following about this:

"The real question does not concern the origin of this right. Neither does it matter what kind of moral arguments we use to defend our standpoint. The only adequate question is whether this right is suitable for making peace in the region or not. It is quite evident at once that this principle is seeking for a proper solution to the confused East-Central European situation. We have mentioned before that the whole territorial confusion of the region stems from the fact that the different nations in this region have become a conglomeration of people using the same language. Therefore, if they wanted to separate these nations in a distinctive way, they had to resort to the principle of linguistic borders and not that of historical borders. The meaning of the right for self-determination would have been to help in reaching a more reasonable arrangement in order to avoid the typical East-Central European situation in which groups of people belong to a historical community that does not correspond to that of their nation. Peoples' right for self-determination would have served as a principle to manifest these transformations in their national affiliation. Unfortunately "peace makers" in 1919 were not able to use this principle, which they accepted in theory in a consequent way and fix the borders in East-Central Europe for the forthcoming centuries. The principle of peoples' right for self-determination was not clearly adjusted to the requirements of the special problems in this region for the solution of which it was meant to be used. And since peace makers felt it a burden upon themselves anyway to use the right for self-determination consequently in every respect and everywhere, they were too happy to give it up. Disregarding these principles had its own consequences and contributed a lot to the development of the policy of **aggression** in Germany and, as a result, to the emergence of Hitler's type of fascism. On the other hand, the latter referred to the principle of self-determination only as a pretext for covering a maniacal, power-oriented policy, which discredited the whole idea in the end."

After the Second World War it was almost forbidden or at least of no use even mentioning this principle for a long time. As we all know, these badly and inconsequently used principles and the "ill-made" peace treaties led our countries to the dead-lock of fierce hostility and blind nationalism. Regarding only the interests and political will of the superpowers, which cover and ignore all the differences in East-Central Europe and which take only the interests and the requirements of the Western European social development into consideration, we cannot understand the situation in this region and cannot find real solutions to our special problems. Remembering the difficulties and the conflicts resulting from

14

the disintegration of the big colonial empires, the West still does not think it advisable and desirable to apply the principle of self-determination in the East-Central European region in an emphatic way. International organizations, especially the members involved are suspicious even today when the principle of the right for self-determination is mentioned. Their attitude is very similar concerning the question of autonomy. Their logic is the following: autonomy equals separatism, separatism leads to secession and causes wars. These notions are perpetually fixed with these labels.

For us here in East-Central Europe, it is quite strange that the viewpoint of the new, Western type of regimes is very close in this respect to that of the ex-communist regimes, which categorically refused all movements towards autonomy saying that it was against the principle of the Bolshevik notion of equality. We have always believed here in this region that it was a specific and inherent characteristic of Bolshevik ideology to refuse any kind of difference, and at the same time any sign of autonomy in the name of equality and in the spirit of uniformity. For these regimes autonomy was equal with independence, which meant decisions independent of central authorities and total lack of control, which were absolutely unacceptable and unbearable for these central powers, because these movements and transitions could have blown up the framework of the whole political structure built on Bolshevism.

However reluctantly we did it, we had to realize after a while that all the different concepts of autonomy conceived in this region after 1989 induced suspicion and uncertainty in the political elite of the newly formed democratic regimes, and most of the time - though not always and not everywhere - international organizations took the same stand on the issue.

II

Liberalization and Autonomy as a Tension Relieving Factor

Accepting the argument that "the history of Yugoslavia is only the history of a continuous postponing of disintegration already written into its history right at the beginning," we can also say that the history of the country may show that the emergence of regional autonomies developing during the process of liberalization could have ceased the tensions originating from its status as an "unaccomplished state" and from the failure to form a nation-state.

Nowadays the different states in the East-Central European region represent different opportunities for a transition to democratic legitimacy. In most of the countries the lack of democratic legitimacy and its consequences push political powers in the direction of nationalistic tendencies.

If democratic legitimacy and the real values of the European civilization - economic prosperity, political and human rights - can manifest themselves and can serve as a framework for society then the demand for independence and various forms of autonomy are to be considered acceptable and a normal political practice. This kind of policy would lessen the pains and troubles resulting from the lack of a political balance and society would not be so vulnerable to political hysteria. The absence or the delayed achievement of a bourgeois type of society and the problems of modernization cannot serve as a pretext to avoid the problems of developing a democratic society.

"Democracy in a way is a system of rules controlling the self-government of society, the main function of which is to lay down the basic rules and regulations and the scope of possibilities determining the relationship of the groups and individuals in society to power. Democracy is based on a free co-operation of independent individuals and on the rational acceptance of the rules controlling it. On the contrary, nation is an organic community based on shared emotions and wills, which determines its members' culture, way of thinking, loyalties within and outside the given community and their relationship with other national communities. Within the boundaries of a nation individual autonomies organize themselves to be a collective will and they struggle to manifest themselves as collective independence and sovereignty. Therefore, democracy and nationhood are principles that can be connected but never substituted with each other", writes Péter Hanák in his introduction to the work of Oscar Jaszi entitled Disintegration of the Habsburg Monarchy.

But in this region new issues cover the old perspectives. Yugoslavia can serve as an extreme example. While "the territory called Yugoslavia was torn apart and ruled by ethnic oligarchies in a feudal way, ... the processes of liberalization were suppressed and the main principles ruling the country were those of a functional distribution of Bolshevik power. In the sixties, when there emerged a possibility to respond to the existing problems in an alternative way, political powers fearing that they would give way to a self-inducing process, judged the dangers of liberalization more serious than those of nationalism, which they thought would be easier to control.... In the seventies and eighties the practice of nationalism was a privilege of the national Bolshevik parties ... which actually served, as they hoped, to keep a "subdued" and "tamed" nationalism under control within the labyrinth of the party organizations ... and not to let the ghost out of the bottle poisoning the uncontrolled part of society. As a result, instead of regionalism, tendencies towards developing a strong national state have become more determining since the seventies. Only in Serbia, the largest republic, have they succeeded in forming two quasi independent autonomies as a result of fierce arguments within the party: Voivodina and Kosovo, where the local party oligarchies gained power..." (Alpár Losoncz; Déja vu on the Balkans)

Today it is quite evident, especially from East-Central Europe, that with the help of the principles of liberalization and autonomy the war could have been avoided.

The question still stands: *Why, even after all these events, are several elite political groups in our region suspicious when the issue of autonomy is to be discussed.*

III

Self-government and Autonomy as a means alien to the System

Nineteenth century traditions do not seem to help a lot in solving the problem since the ideal of a homogenous type of nation-state cannot be followed in the present situation. It is almost impossible to establish the same number of small states as the number of different ethnic groups that live in this region, not to mention the nationalities living geographically scattered and interspersed. Neither can any version of a Bolshevik type of solution be a real answer to these challenges since they only sweep the problems under the carpet pretending no conflicts exist. This method did not work anywhere, both in Yugoslavia and the Soviet Union it proved to be completely useless and inefficient.

What other possibilities are there? Let's examine the real cause and effect relationship first.

Is it the case that the post-socialist countries of the region are poor, their economic and social structures are underdeveloped, they lack a sufficient amount of capital and the institutions of democracy and a constitutional state are not working efficiently because they have substantial minorities? I think the answer is clearly and unambiguously negative. Then we have to raise the question: will tendencies toward assimilation or ethnic purges solve the real issues of these countries? The answer is again negative of course.

In that case we should not give ourselves to a complete inertia and let events move in this direction. I trust it is evident for everybody that these countries are in this situation because of their delayed achievement of a bourgeois type of society, because they are in different stages of economic, historical, political and cultural development, and not because of their minorities. The inertia and immobility, the rigidity and inflexibility of the past forty years had their own effect on our recent history and our recent possibilities.

The principle of territorial integrity is another question that is in close connection with the issue. What is the rationale for equating territorial integrity with a unitary or centralized form of government? Our experiences here in East-Central Europe prove it clearly that a government's emphasis on territorial integrity is merely a smokescreen to cover up its unwillingness to share political power. Hurst Hannum writes in his book entitled Autonomy, Sovereignty, and Self-Determination, published in Philadelphia in 1990 that:

"federal or consociational states, or those in which substantial powers have been devolved to local governments are

19

[not] any less sovereign or stable than unitary states: in fact, the reverse may be true".

He continues:

"Territory can be seen as a primary guarantor of two fundamental human needs, identity and security."

And, as he writes, most of the time

"...it is gross violations of human rights that commonly create a minority's need, which may not be present in earlier stages of a conflict, for a specific territorial base or homeland".

That is why - to avoid the development of these conflicts - it is important to emphasize that

"the creation of representative local government structures is fundamental to most demands for autonomy".

He also examines what guidance may be found in international legal principles towards identifying a core of values which might be included in a "right to autonomy" and argues that

"self-determination may be exercised by a people in any manner it freely chooses, from full integration with an existing state to total independence. ... Many new actors - from individuals to transnational corporations to sub-state and inter-state entities - have acquired varying degrees of international personality, and [he adds] international law is developing, if with some hesitation, sufficient flexibility to accommodate them".

He also finds it important that:

"where demands for autonomy and self-determination are asserted as a matter of right, they are often founded on the illegitimacy of the government or the state itself".

After 1989 there were free general elections in almost all of the states in the region. Nevertheless, even if we examine only one, though a very important factor, namely the question of separation of powers, we must see that this principle for example, which is of vital importance in a democratic society is far from being applied or respected according to its importance - though in different ways and different degrees - and in some countries even its grounds are questioned. And then we have not even mentioned the informal political sub-structures, the parties, different interest groups, the media, etc. The working of Western type democracies show that these elements all have their own functions in a subtly built-up, well-differentiated and well-organized system and the way they work is just as important and determining from the point of view of the operation of the system as distribution of power itself. Where political parties and different interest groups do not form well-differentiated, autonomous sub-systems and where the autonomy of the media is little or uncertain, then the system itself becomes instable. When the system is instable, all the means aiming at solving the minority issue, economic, organizational and cultural autonomies, self-government, etc. will become and remain alien bodies in the system and will only enhance frustration and cause more conflicts.

IV

Possibilities of a Breakthrough
Where are the possibilities to break out of this situation?

What are the conditions that are conducive to cooperation between the elite and the stable non elite support and that make the situation of different groups within society manageable? According to Arend Lijphart the following factors appear to be particularly important in this respect:

1) A multiple balance of power between different groups of society.
2) Confidence of the whole society.
3) Segmental isolation.
4) The elit should have the ability to adapt and compromise.

It is inevitable to ask the question: Where are we in this respect?

Our future depends on how much the different political powers in the region can get over the old-fashioned idea of a homogenous and paternalist national state and how much they can understand and accept - in their own interests - the necessity and the importance of supporting the development of various types of autonomies. There is no other way, since these autonomies are necessary pre-conditions for a healthy economic and social development without which it is impossible to move towards modernization or build up a stable power with efficient legislative, executive and juridical authorities.

Today, most of the minorities in the region, are forced into a position where they have to feel the threat of total assimilation or where they get involved in different aggressive, nationalist feelings, either as aggressors or victims. If they are lucky enough, they will not be the followers of the Basque, the Catalonian or the Irish methods and will not get involved in a tragedy like the one in Yugoslavia. But to avoid all these

22

dangers, we have to understand that the only possibility for us is to recognize our common interests, and to cooperate and consociate.

To realize these possibilities means a very difficult and long process during which minorities and majorities have to make consensus day by day; it is not enough to accept these ideas, they have to become real and they have to be incorporated in political will and reality. Even if both sides have a positive approach to this question and both really wish to solve this problem, it needs long and patient cooperation based on consequent work and mutual understanding for decades. It is not impossible; nowadays we can see some examples of this. For instance, the Palestinian-Israeli conflict seems to find a way in establishing an autonomous Palestinian territory. But we can also think of the Spanish model or the case of South Tyrol, etc. It required decades to resolve these cases as well.

To summarize, I think that, although, movements towards autonomy in this region sometimes, depending on the state and stage of democracy in a given country, seem to be alien to the whole political and social system, on the whole, these tendencies are to the advantage of society and change social development in a positive way. Most of the time the local "majority" society seems to be over-suspicious when minority groups are talking about self-government and autonomy. We can relieve these tensions and prevent civil wars in the region only if we approach these questions in an open-minded and very differentiated way, trying to learn and understand all the viewpoints and the interests behind them and endeavour to conceive the real content of these tendencies, fighting against our suspicion- and fear-driven prejudices. On the other hand, we have a great task ahead of us: it would be urgent to devise the typology of the movements towards autonomy in this region; it could be a great help in the work of international organizations and other forums.

I would like to end with the same motto I started my essay with, but in a modified version. In this transitional period of time, in the changing societies of East-Central Europe "the possibilities of choosing political activities are limited," therefore we have to be open to all the possible solutions that have proved their positive effect on social development during history. Movements towards autonomy seem to be one of these.

Towards a Knowledge Based Society
Gábor Kolumbán

Not long ago the draft of a new law on "National Minorities and Self-governing Communities" was adopted in Marosvásárhely by the Council of District Representatives in the Hungarian Democratic Alliance of Romania (HDAR). Actually, this was the final step of a more than two year long theoretical debate among the competing groups, ideas and approaches concerning the issue of autonomy within the HDAR.

Being the result of a concensus, the proposed solution and the accepted version of the Bill seem to be appropriate to serve as a base of negotiations between the Hungarian side and the decisive segments of the social and political life in Romania. In my opinion, in the present situation - after adopting Romania's membership in the Council of Europe - none of the responsible political powers can avoid taking a stand on the minority issue and giving their opinion on the HDAR's proposal.

The HDAR was established in December 1989, directly after the crucial political turn in Romania. The Alliance, being the representative and protective organization of the Hungarian national minority interests in Romania, has a definite programme to defend all the rightful demands and expectations of the Hungarian community, the meeting of which could assure the assertion of the Hungarian national identity and could provide all the institutions indispensable for the community to have a healthy economic and cultural development. They demand to have the full range of public institutions that could provide education in their native language at all levels - including the reestablishment of Bolyai University - they claim to have the right to use the Hungarian language in administration and justice and desire a total financial restitution of the historical Hungarian churches and cultural institutions as well as demanding a wide-ranging political representation in Parliament and administration.

In the beginning the HDAR had a traditionally liberal policy in a sense: they raised all their issues from the point of view of general human and minority rights and they considered it to be the government's task to solve them. After long decades of the coercive paternalism of a communist dictatorship, the Hungarian politicians in Romania were shocked to experience hostility and a forceful social and political resistance from the side of the Romanians when they tried to vindicate their claims and demands and put them into practice. When we say this, we especially refer to such events as those which took place in March 1990 in Marosvásárhely, the debates in Parliament on the Hargita-Kovászna Report and the new Constitution and the constitutional statutes legitimizing the new nation-state and their practical consequences in governing the country.

When nationalist Romanian parties gained power, the HDAR felt compelled to change its basic strategy. Instead of emphasising the traditional values and purposes mentioned above, they shifted the stress to more constructive forms of self-organization. The crucial moments in this respect were the following: the Kolozsvár Declaration of October 1992 and the Congress of Brassó in January 1993. The importance of these events was that it was the first time when the Hungarian community could express its political demand for autonomy and for the institutions of self-government in a clear-cut way. At the same time they gave voice to their wish to begin taking up political dialogue with the progressive elements of Romanian political life and start negotiations in accordance with the principles of the Gyulafehérvár Declaration in 1918, which promised to grant autonomy to all nations in Transylvania. We always try to do our best within the limits of legality to provide both the political and financial backgrounds and the necessary public authorities to assure the work of the institutions of autonomy.

Since this is a conference organized by a liberal party, the Free Democratic Alliance and my liberal friends from Romania are bound to respond to the same problems, I suggest the approach mentioned above to avoid a row of unfruitful debates on the superiority and preference of individual versus collective rights, which is a very artificial and unproductive contradiction and leads nowhere as far as practical solutions are concerned. At the same time I hope I can make all the participants here understand why the solution of the minority issue enjoys preference in the policy of the HDAR to the general issues of democracy and market economy and serves as an indispensable precondition to asking real questions about them, even if this approach apparently makes it more difficult to negotiate with the potential political partners in society.

In my opinion, the stand the HDAR has recently taken on this issue is in accordance with the requirements of our time. We hope it offers a solution that might be an answer to one of the most serious and tension-raising issues of our century and probably the next one as well. The main question is: how is it possible for communities with different identity to live together in peaceful co-existence in such a way that these individuals belonging to the same state may live in security as equal citizens and at the same time can assert their identity without having to feel that they are second-rate citizens and without being discriminated against for their identity.

I did not determine the identity that creates a

community. I did it on purpose. In modern societies individuals have a lot of different identities and national and language identities represent only one - though in the present day East-Central European countries probably the most important - form of individuality.

It must be quite clear from the aforementioned statements that in my opinion we should - as far as possible - shift emphasis from general human and minority rights and the problems of self-determination to the questions of how different communities can live a relatively independent life governing their own issues in peaceful co-existence. This is a clearly practical approach, which instead of referring to the people's right of self-determination - might it be "natural" or "historical" - follows a more pragmatic and functionalist way of thinking and using the present situation as a starting point it puts more emphasis on questions like that of autonomy, self-administration and the institutions of self-government. I am fully convinced that the claims and demands of the Hungarian community in Romania remain unheard not because they cannot be accepted but because there is no political will to realize them. I do not wish to go into details now, I only refer to the question of Bolyai University or that of the Hungarian Consulate in Kolozsvár. At the same time we know a lot of groupings and cases of status quo - especially local or regional non-organizational forms - which though they lack any formal and legal base, have deeply rooted living traditions and have been working for centuries. In my opinion, we should try and find solutions taking the following principles into consideration:

1) The solution must be coherent legally and has to fit organically into the framework of the given state.

2) The solution must be acceptable politically and must be supported by a wide range of society. Minority interests cannot be asserted without the support of the majority society and its policy.
3) The solution must be viable in such a way that it can be executed and which is quite sure to work and sustain, provided all the indispensable professional, financial and organizational conditions are given

There is another axiom that has to be taken seriously to provide all these conditions in safe circumstances, namely respect for the principles of the status quo, the principle that the existing borders are immutable.

As we can see, there are only long processes and no overnight solutions. Taking the special situation in Romania as a starting point, the proposal of the HDAR makes a functional difference between the various national minorities according to the degree of organization and considering how much demand and competence they have to manage their own issues. The principle of internal self-determination is actually the extension of the principle of subsidiarity to other forms of communities, which was originally used in connection with the autonomy of different local communities and which is a well-known and accepted idea in European thinking. The principle of subsidiarity - as it was laid down in the European Charter of Local Self-Governments, an agreement adopted by the Council of Europe in 1985 - is a functional principle that makes it possible to distribute powers and abilities according to the principles of democracy and the decentralization of power. Under article 3 in Chapter 4 of the Charter we can read the following: "As a rule, matters of public interests must be decided on at a level of administration most available for the citizens.

Devolution of these tasks upon other administrative authorities fully depends on the nature of the issue and might be possible for economic and other reasons of efficiency."

Article 4 lays down the following: "As a rule, local authorities have full and exclusive power in these issues. These rights can be restricted by other, central or regional authorities only by force of law."

Obviously, local communities consist of the inhabitants of a given area. The coherence of a local community is based on the local citizens' common interests and identity. Local communities are actually autonomous ones and in each case they exercise their autonomy according to the principle of subsidiarity. The authority of a local self-government stems from two different sources: on the one hand, central authorities devolve a part of their responsibility on the authorities of local or regional autonomous communities; on the other hand, there are numerous local issues that must belong to the competence of these local authorities because the nature of the matters at hand require so.

The questions of devolution and decentralization of power have always been and will always be sore political points in every society throughout history, especially in societies like the present Romania, where the nation-state has an extremely strong central power. Unitary systems are apt to interpret decentralization tendencies as hostile attacks against the state or as a restriction or offence of its sovereignty and they will never see them as a means to manage different public issues in a more efficient and economical way, which better serve the interests of the citizens. Unfortunately, recent "administration wars" between the newly established local and regional self-governments and the central powers, especially the central government in Romania - and all the other countries of East-

Central Europe I suppose - painfully demonstrate the truth of my statements. The main difficulty in decentralizing power lies in the fact that stemming from the very nature of autonomy itself, these autonomous communities and their self-governing institutions must have a co-ordinate and never a subordinate relationship with each other. There is no other way to make the system of autonomy work.

The principle of subsidiarity is of crucial importance because it can serve as a perfect means to separate and decentralize power and build up a dynamic hierarchy of authorities according to competence and the nature of the problems. The principle of subsidiarity is a deconstructive principle which makes it possible to break down the centralized system of administration. It distributes vertically organized competencies into horizontal ones in a way that at the same time preserves the level of integrity in the whole system. If we apply this principle in a consequential way, we can control the system changing processes necessary for our times in a way that the increase of the internal complexity of the social system will involve the increase of the level of social integrity and as a result this process will lead to a dynamic stability and to the falling apart of the whole system. There are several deplorable political consequences of the fact that here in the East-Central European region our politicians - unlike the ones in the democratic societies of the West - did not realize how important this principle was. They could not recognize that the principle of subsidiary was one of the greatest intellectual achievements of political thinking in our time, which could help to lead us peacefully from our industrialized society to a post-industrialized social system based on knowledge.

The survival of old, nineteenth century political structures and mechanisms have pushed our region to the periphery in the strong competition of modernization. Is it possible that the big loser at the turn of the century will be the same again, that is East-Central Europe?

Communities, especially the autonomous ones play a basic role in determining the security and the chances of modernization for the citizens of a given country. Autonomous communities are needed because their institutions are the most available for the local people and they give the best opportunity for citizens to control authority in a direct way. Another great advantage is that they provide a fertile environment for culture to blossom and for local human resources to use their energies very efficiently.

The existence and the development of a community and the assertion of its individual characteristics is of essential importance from the individuals' point of view as well. Actually, it is a basic individual interest of everybody. On the other hand, the right of all citizens to form efficient local communities to meet their basic demands is a basic human right. In a knowledge based society cultural and informational demands will be the most determining. Opposing the idea of community rights, a lot of liberal thinkers in the region support the extremely popular idea of a minimal state, but actually they do not follow through and cannot judge the consequences. It is a fact, that a unitary state usually cannot manage public affairs in an efficient and economical way, but we have to admit that this is partly because the number and the complexity of these issues are increasing. When we restrict the state we have to find institutions that can take these responsibilities. We cannot restrict the state just for the sake of restriction; these tasks must be executed somehow. The existence of local communities is of vital importance in this respect, since these institutions can shoulder the responsibilities and solve the problems in an efficient way in their areas.

Going back to the HDAR's proposal, it is quite clear now that it is actually a political question that while the Romanian authorities do not question the autonomy of different religious and local communities, they are vehemently against any signs of autonomy as far as language, culture or ethnic identity are concerned. They do not accept the national minorities' right to use their own language in education and in administration. The main reason of this strict refusal is that with these rights minorities could gain more knowledge and information, which is obviously not desirable. I do not think I am mistaken when I predict that we can expect a long struggle and not only for rights but also for culture-specific resources. The institutional system of a given community is always quite a reliable index for judging the level of integrity and organization. Provided a community intends to arrange its own matters autonomously it needs special public authorities to set up its own institutional system to execute these tasks. Actually, a community can gain autonomy through the institution of self-government, or at least we can say that self-government is a minimal requirement and an indispensable precondition of autonomy.

Article 3 of the Local Autonomy Charter determines the notion of self-government in the following way:

> 1) Local self-government means the rights and the actual possibilities of local authorities to manage and control most public issues especially those of local interests within the framework of administrative regulations in the region.
> 2) The right of self-government can be exercised by councils and assemblies the members of which are

elected by a free, secret and direct general election and which have executive bodies accountable to them.

After the definition, let us have a closer look at the characteristics of self-government:

1) Self-governments are factors of power. In the case of local self-governments it practically means the devolution of the state administrative powers to local and regional powers, with all the necessary authorities and local statuses of power. The importance of self-governments as power-forming factors is always determined by the result of a long political fight and debate between centralizing and decentralizing tendencies, which is then laid down in laws reflecting this balance.

2) Independence and institutional autonomy, which are guaranteed by the following factors:

- constitutional protection of these rights and authorities; guaranteeing exclusive rights in their own competence

- personal properties and rights to control their economic matters

- cooperative relations with other autonomies

- outside supervision might concern only legality and must be regulated by law

3) Relationship with the community, direct control, openness.

Self-governing is a democratic way of organization, decision-makers are elected by general, direct and secret elections. Decision making and executive powers are separated and are directly subordinated to the community. This way the institutional interests of a self-government are dependent on the interests of the community in a direct way.

Considering the characteristics mentioned above the self-government of an autonomous community can be placed somewhere between the institutions of the state and the civil society. Being a public power with different administrative authorities it is closer to the state, but its autonomy, close and organic relations with the community and its local character makes it more similar to the institutions of civil society. According to Savelsberg, locality means a system of special interests and values fighting against outer influences. It always involves a special system of symbols that help to lead the community's life, as well as a kind of constellation of people and groups whose special local values and political interests strongly influence the community and who rely on specific local material resources and exchange values. Locality, if it is associated with autonomy, provides a strong feeling of security for the individuals.

The criteria mentioned above can be applied easily to describe other kinds of communities (language, ethnic, religious), which - similar to local communities - express a special kind of affiliation. Thus, we can use a unified conceptual framework to describe the whole group of phenomena, we can have a common denominator to discuss different communal self-governments and their relations and co-operation.

The great advantage of the HDAR's minority proposals is that they regulate the concept of communal autonomy in a legally coherent way.

Let me describe the concept of regional autonomy in a few words, because it illustrates very well how self-governments with different identities can co-operate with each other. Since the proposal is careful enough not to claim that in territories where national minority communities are greater in number, the institutions of regional autonomy equal to the representation of special minority interests, it can easily avoid a futile debate about autonomy. Minority interests should infiltrate through the institutions of regional autonomy: it means bilinguality, communication and discussions with the ethnic self-governments, the right to veto, etc. This solution is remarkable because it avoids restricting the inner sovereignty of the nation-state within the country and by involving all the ethnic groups in the territory according to the principle of ethnicity and by taking a common responsibility, it strengthens the stability of the state. Self-governments with special status can achieve regional autonomy as a result of democratic elections at local level and are free to associate and co-operate with other (ethnic or non-ethnic) autonomous communities' self-governments to assert and represent their interests. It provides a large scope to arrange public affairs in an autonomous way with large liberty taking all the differences and special characteristics into account.

Finally, let me express my conviction that this attempt to solve the main problems of national and other types of minorities through the institutions of communal self-governments and regional autonomies is an organic part of the whole process of the quick and steady development of self-help organizations. These attempts reflect a strong wish to take a direct and active part in our own life and govern it, to determine our own selves, to emancipate ourselves and to take responsibility for our actions and our future and autonomy can add a lot to it. The realization of the proposals mentioned above is greatly dependent on the whole restructuring process of society, which involves accepting the concept of self-government and establishing the institutions of autonomy parallel to those of the constitutional state and democracy.

Owing exactly to the weakness and underdevelopment of the constitutional state as an institution, demands for communal self-governments appear much stronger and intensely in East-Central Europe than in the West.

As we can see, as a result of this process there might develop a special network of relationships in the region, at least in places where there are a substantial number of ethnic minorities and they determine themselves as autonomous communities.

Provided new nation-states in the region can accept this challenge and try to use these creative energies to modernize, they will build up a kind of non-territorial democracy.

The Autonomy Conception of the Hungarian Democratic Community of Voivodina General Principles for Analysis

András Á goston

The fundamental principles of the Hungarian Democratic Community of Voivodina (HDCV) published under the title of Hungarian Autonomy - similar to any other significant document - can be analysed in several ways. It was published more than a year ago and it has had its own effect on several important fields of social and political life. Three of them are worth having a closer look at in a bit more detail.

The HDCV's conception of autonomy as a basic political document is principal especially from the point of view of the Hungarian minority in Voivodina. It proves that this native group of people - in spite of a period of more than seventy years of drawbacks in its history as a minority - is able to organize itself if the conditions and the historical possibilities are favourable. It has established an effective organization, which is built up in an upward hierarchy according to the basic principles of democracy and which is able to represent the political interests of the group efficiently. In accordance with the principle of democracy it has worked out its legitimacy, it has a distinct image of the future and a clear-cut programme how to assure the Hungarian national minority in Voivodina the rights for autonomy, which serves as an indispensable legal condition to assert and manifest national identity. Two other factors make these results even more significant, so important actually, that we can surely regard this event as a turning point in the history of the Hungarian minority in Voivodina. Firstly, these principles were drafted and adopted by the annual assembly of the HDCV during a period of fierce clashes when the organization and the whole Hungarian community were the target of unleased Serbian political terror. Secondly, these principles had been adopted and thus legitimized twice by an overwhelming majority of voters during the parliamentary elections. The document represents the beginning of a new era. From this time on the organization can become an active political factor and an independent actor on the stage of politics. Hopefully, if the historical conditions are favourable it might be able to survive in the forthcoming century.

This political document is of historic importance from the point of view of the whole Hungarian community all over the world. Although, none of the Hungarian national minority groups raise the issue of borders in the Carpathian Basin, the minority issue of the Hungarian nationalities is still an open and unsolved problem and a challenge for democracy in the East-Central European region. Since the demands of the Hungarian minority group in Voivodina are well-defined and put down in clear-cut political documents, they can be presented at different international forums and they can serve as a good example for other Hungarian minority groups for autonomy in a democratic way. In the present political situation it is a necessity for the legitimate factors of the Hungarian nationalities in the different East-Central European countries to cooperate and unite their forces. The well-defined demands drawn up in the autonomy conception of the HDCV do not confine the sovereignty of the state but at the same time serve as a legal framework to assure that the national identity of the minority may preserve and manifest itself. This way the Hungarian government, which tries to support the minority issues and cooperate with the Hungarian minority groups in the neighbouring countries, can minimize the risk of being charged with too much commitment and involvement. At the same time, taking the initiative there are more chances that the models aiming at defending the Hungarian minorities' rights in a more effective way might get a more favourable acceptance at different international forums and this way the general advantage for the whole of the Hungarian community all over the world can be maximized.

The autonomy conception of the HDCV has already been regarded as an important political document at different international forums. Not only because it has already happened that a state has assured minority rights to its own national minorities on the basis of these principles and has followed the mechanism "prescribed" in these documents. More important is the fact that the autonomy conception of the HDCV can be an integral part of a more and more acceptable international trend which tries to transform the whole economic and political structures of the East-Central European countries and make them market oriented societies. Regarding the fact that a market economy cannot be effective without the smooth operation of a democratic political system, establishing such states has become a primary task in this region for the whole of the international political community. All the more, because it has become very evident during the past few years that these transitions towards democracy are not easy at all in any of the ex-socialist countries. But that is not all. Now everybody must see it - even if he or she does not want to - that it is impossible to establish democratic regimes in these states without solving and closing the unresolved and open minority issues in a democratic way. There are several signs that the autonomy model of the HDCV is in full accordance with the international trend mentioned above. The political compromise that the conception offers seems to fit into the main currents since, on the one hand, it respects the principle of territorial integrity, it does not want to change any borders and, on the other hand, it is a viable model to assure national minorities to preserve their national identity. The model can become a general formula to be followed in the region. There is more and more evidence that international organizations should support this model for security reasons as well.

To summarize: the importance of the autonomy conception of the HDCV as a political document cannot be simplified and it cannot be said that its only merit and advantage is that it provides a legal framework for assuring nationality rights for the minorities and making them possible to preserve and manifest their national identity. It also serves general Hungarian interests and contributes to help the whole national community solve their problems and take steps to achieve the goal of joining a European community by solving its minority issues in a democratic way. Finally, the autonomy conception of the HDCV offers a compromise that can be considered to be the first step in the direction of finding solutions to more general problems that cannot be settled without arranging minority issues in a democratic way.

Secondly, the autonomy conception of the HDCV can be appreciated as a new constitutional incentive. The document itself contains several elements of a strong demand to define the principle and institution of autonomy in a constitutional way, but it is more of a political than of legal importance. The triple autonomy conception can also be regarded as a model of a democratic method of decentralization, since even the Serbian constitution in force makes it possible for the central authorities to invest a part of their rights to other institutions, especially to local self-governments. In this case, the principle of autonomy would lack the right for legislative power. We must say however, that in the present situation the demand to corporate the right for autonomy in the constitution is indispensable to settle a series of political problems, calm down and relieve the tensions and build up a a good relationship between the Hungarian national minority in Voivodina and the central Serbian authorities. We have to mention however, that the autonomy conception of the HDCV in its present form is actually only a draft list of legal provisions to corporate the minority's political demands in a compact form. It can get a final, more refined form only as a result of a long negotiation process between the HDCV and the central authorities. Nevertheless, the main principles are essential and they cannot be an issue of negotiation.

Thirdly, the autonomy conception of the HDCV, especially after having possibilities to set up local self-governments with HDCV majority and after the almost total destruction and disintegration of the entire educational and cultural system and the media, can also be considered to be a political base for the building of the new regime, which is just coming into existence with lots of pain and suffering. The Hungarian government's financial support to cover a part of the expenses of different Hungarian educational and cultural institutions and the media in Voivodina, can be sufficient to lay down the base of the institutions of a future self-government, and sometimes even to develop them, on the condition that we are aware of this double function of these institutions and we make efforts to develop them in this direction. At the local self-governments, where the representatives of the HDCV are in a majority, we can start building up favourable conditions for a territorial autonomy.

The first part of the sentence is unfortunately more emphatic, that is, we can start doing it, even if we cannot hope too much in the present situation, when due to lack of reasonable compromises with the Serbian authorities, there are too many obstacles and because of severe political pressures there are too few brave and original initiatives and purpose oriented and competent activities. In spite of this, even under these pressures and difficult conditions we can always practise democracy and try to learn and behave according to the principles of a constitutional state and a democratic civil society. We can always try to take and hold responsibility and start working within these pseudo-conditions and structures of autonomy. It is of vital importance to have the first experiences in how to operate multi-national self-governments. It is very important from political point of view that these first experiments of cooperation (or clashes) within the local self-governments make the principle of autonomy acceptable (or unacceptable) for the Serbian side. Cooperation - or even the conflicts and the development of conflict-solving mechanisms can do a good service to demystify the notion of autonomy, which has been demonized by the media. All this entails a relief of tensions, which can be beneficial and prepare the dialogue between the minority groups and the central powers. Although there are self-governments even in settlements, where the nationalities live geographically scattered, partly due to some special regulations of the local self-government still in force and partly because of strong political pressures from outside they have not really become conscious and self-confident representatives and supporters of the minority interests in the local governments. Nevertheless, all the rules and regulations and all the formal and informal "tricks" of making policy and political decisions can be learnt and these local representatives of democracy will surely do so in the near future. This way the local conditions are going to be more and more favourable for the conception of the idea of autonomy.

Civil Society and National Power
Tibor Várady

Like in a caricature, all the main issues and tendencies of our time are reflected in an extreme way in the distorted mirror of Yugoslavia's social and political life. The picture is more cruel and drastic in this mirror, but at the same time, it reveals the true nature of the East-Central European countries more clearly and lucidly, because it attracts our attention to the most essential and most characteristic features of these societies without any veil or cover. The abnormal and extreme enhancement of national identity and the suppression and destruction of any other national identity resulted in such an escalation that naturally led to war. When ethnicity becomes an above-all criterion then minority issues always get a dramatic overtone and the fate and the existence of different minority communities - those who are fewer in number in a given area - always becomes insecure and questionable.

It is very important to see this problem in an economic context. When economic criteria are really dominant in a society, members of a minority group will take their place in society more or less according to their economic resources and their expertise. More or less I say, because of course there are no absolute measurements. But when ethnicity has to be the main criterion of whether to employ an engineer or not, it is very difficult to take economic reasons and mechanisms into consideration. It is a real danger of course - and we cannot ignore it - that by interpreting the problem in this way we might put two nation-states - a big one and a small one - on different sides of the battlefield. There is no doubt, though, that when measurements are so biased and tendencies so distorted we cannot leave it for economy and the rules of civil life to decide the fate of minorities. In such a context - but in others as well - struggles for autonomy are a completely understandable and legitimate demand, which can give us some hope for a real solution. I agree with Erika Törzsök when she claims that in our societies autonomy as a means is alien to the system and when I say this I mean all kinds of autonomy, not only national or minority autonomy. The concept of autonomy itself means a kind of devolution, distribution and decentralization of power. From this point of view unitary states fighting for absolute power always feel threatened by ethnical, regional, professional, or any other forms of autonomy. That is why I think that in theory the idea of autonomy - all kinds of autonomy including the one we are talking about here - can do a lot to make our civil life less strained.

Yugoslavia seems to be an ideal place to examine the problems of collective rights because these phenomena are more crystallized there. Discrimination is painfully extensive, hundreds and thousands of people are exterminated just because they belong to a certain group. They have no other sins, they are killed because they are Bosnian Muslims and not Serbs, or they are Serbs and not Muslims; Croatians kill Serbs and Serbs kill Croatians. I mention these nations because they are playing the main roles now, but it is not their special ethnical characteristic. The same phenomena can be experienced in any other country, among any other ethnic group - including Hungarians, of course - provided the historical circumstances are favourable for that. The problem that people are discriminated against just because they belong to a certain ethnic group, cannot be solved at a general human rights level. We live in such an age and atmosphere when even such extremely individual cases as sexual violence will take on an ethnic overtone and will become the means or rather the projection of ethnical fundamentalism somehow. It is very difficult to build up a defence system when we do not know the target of offence. In this case groups of people and minority communities have become the target of offence. If this fact is ignored, it is very difficult to build up a defence system. Thirty years ago, when the very sore issue of the Blacks was raised in the American Supreme Court, they had to decide whether to defend Black rights as basic individual human rights, or as collective rights, and whether to use some kind of positive discrimination. In a decision in 1963 the Supreme Court went "against the flow" in a way and took a very clear stand on the issue supporting the latter version and put it down straight that if we wish to solve racial problems, we cannot ignore the race itself. There is no other way. When the existence of groups and whole communities are at stake, it is very difficult to work out an adequate defence system without taking the ethnic aspects into consideration, and if we do so we have to get to the problem of collective rights. When talking about this issue, it is very important to find some kind of principles whether individual or collective rights are concerned. It is of crucial importance to find unbiased, generally applicable measures. We should try and find collective rights that are valid everywhere, or at least in this region where these problems were generated. Thus, especially in Yugoslavia, but in other East-Central European countries as well, we should find measures that are valid for all minority groups. There will always be differences of course. For example the Ruthenian minority cannot have an independent university in Yugoslavia, but the Albanians or the Hungarians might have one. The Hungarian national minority might not have its own university in the Czech Republic, but they can have one in Slovakia. It is possible for the Serbs to

47

have their own university in Croatia, but not in Hungary for example, but they have the right to have primary and secondary schools in Hungary as well. It is a simple matter of ratio in a given country, but most of the issues are very similar or just as simple. In most cases it is very important to settle issues according to the principle of reciprocity. It is of vital importance, because when making a minority law we somehow ignore the issue of collective rights, the same way as we question the general validity of individual human rights when we negotiate with individuals one by one. Collective rights must be asserted somehow, that is why it is so important that the HDAR submitted a proposal concerning the rights of all minorities in Romania. At the same time, the proposal has tried to reckon with the potential differences as well. That is exactly what we would need in Yugoslavia even in a more comprehensive way if possible.

Zsolt Németh made a statement today which I completely agree with, namely that the idea of autonomy could and should be an important element of Liberalism. I can accept this statement provided that pluralism does not restrict itself to the ethnic aspects of autonomy, may they be minority or majority structures. It would be extremely dangerous from the point of view of any minority group, since a minority structure requires pluralism for its very existence. If a minority structure is prevailing it is of vital importance for the survival of the community to have pluralism. If it were not so, everybody who does not fit in this structure would fall out of his nation as well. That is why it is extremely dangerous to reduce ethnicity to a single structure. Pluralism has to step forward and go beyond the boundaries of ethnicity and nationality. It is essential, since the existence of a community might depend on it. It is very important to conceive the idea of autonomy and work out and organize its institutions, but we must always keep in mind how dangerous it might be to base a system on homogeneous ideas. In that case we might make the blunt mistake of simply confronting a small nation-state with a big one. We have to step beyond the obsolete idea of a nation-state, we have to find something better than that. We have to work out the possibilities of a society where all kinds of autonomies can blossom and prosper, no matter what kind they are, ethnic or other.

Liberalism and Autonomy
László Vógel

I am not a professional politician, so let me start with a "literary" example. I can well imagine a person who belongs to a minority group in Romania, Serbia, or anywhere else in the region and who takes a very active role in his minority community, but at the same time he is a member of a Liberal party in the given country. I think this figure would be an East-Central European Faust, who has two souls to struggle with. It is a futile effort in this region to try and patch the concepts of individual human rights and collective rights together. We will not be able to resolve this contradiction and stop the conflicts between them until we have thoroughly examined all aspects of the problem. We have to talk about these issues, especially at Liberal forums like this. Actually, even today, when their balance is still very insecure we feel the desire and the necessity to fit these two ideas together and bring them into harmony somehow. Right before the war broke out, in response to the Serbian demands of regional autonomy in Krajina, General Tudjman gave a very definite statement at the newly established, freely elected Croatian Parliament clearly refusing these demands. Regional autonomy and minority autonomy were out of the question. His reasoning was not without any lesson: he assured everybody that he decided to do so not because he was against the Serbs, but because he was a convinced Liberal thinker. If individual human rights are guaranteed for everybody - and the Croatian Constitution does guarantee these rights - why need regional autonomy? At the same time he defined Croatia as a nation-state. That was the point when the representatives left the meeting of course and soon the war broke out. It does not mean the war would not have broken out without this, but it is certain that it would not have continued the way it did.

Slobodan Milosevic, another "great Liberal thinker", even managed to have it declared in the Serbian Constitution that by definition Serbia is a community of citizens. He claims that in Serbia each citizen is equal and everybody has equal rights and chances when for example applying for a job. Individual human rights have become a means of manipulation and abuse of power and the division of Liberals.

It is not true that the different minority demands for autonomy in East-Central Europe have been inspired and inflamed by the mother countries or by other outside stimulation; they sprang to life as a response to the post-communist regimes, to the newly organized nation-states. I often try to convince my liberal Serbian friend that from strategical point of view it is not advantageous to attack and criticize minority autonomy. They should create a liberal state first and then minorities will not need autonomy, the whole issue of minority autonomy will be a "tea party". I think it is an unacceptable and sinful luxury that Liberal thinkers oppose the idea of minority autonomy in East-Central Europe, because it gives the impression that they find these tendencies more dangerous than the strong nationalistic tendencies experienced in a lot of places or the unifying and centralizing, etatist tendencies of the nation-state. At this point they seem to be a bit disoriented. Minority groups respond to this behaviour by demanding autonomy. During the Communist era there was regional autonomy in Serbia, but the number of the minority communities rapidly decreased. It is not an invention by Milosevic. It is interesting to see that minority groups refer to general European values in every respect as well - except for one thing, namely a nation's rights. We always refer to such examples as Finland or the South Tyrol, but we tend to forget about the fact that these countries are governed by well-defined, clear laws rather than the spirit of autonomy or the wishes of the minority groups. Finland is an excellent example in this respect, because it is exceptionally well-regulated. The idea of autonomy is well-spread in the region and it usually appeared as a means of defence. Is it possible that it will simply be a victim of a contradiction: autonomies will come to life when they are not needed so much any longer? At the moment they are badly needed: they can serve as an efficient mobilizing power and through their mechanisms we can develop a kind of inside power and a certain ability to resist. Parallel to the slow but steady development of liberalism in the region the possibilities of autonomy are growing as well. I think there are special areas that the concepts of autonomy in use are not able to cover. One of these areas is that of economy. Is it not possible that with the growth of market economy strong unitary states will fall into their own trap? The idea of autonomy has great possibilities in the field of communication or education but regarding cultural life I am not convinced that it does any good. Even today, I can see some tendencies that seem to work against the development of a multi-cultural system. Instead of becoming a mobile nervous-system of the region, minorities are unfortunately getting more and more dependent on the mother countries in the sense that they expect all the positive impulses from them.

These are very important political thoughts, but everyday life is different and cannot be organized according to these rules and ideas. What can we do with mixed marriages, for example? How can they be categorized then? Industrial development and modernization involve the increase of mobility and then autonomy might serve as a mechanism of exclusiveness since it cannot do anything with categories that are mixed or hybrid . It is a real danger that on one hand, these hybrid zones will get farther from economy and on the other hand, as soon as possible, cultural relationships will transform autonomies into lovely "bunches of flowers" without any roots. I think it is important to see these contradictions even if our main concerns are just the opposite today: we are much more worried about politicians who are against the idea of autonomy than about those who support it - at least here in the East-Central European region.

The Model of Decentralization
Mihály Szecsei

Being an economist I might be expected to give you a definite picture of the financial base of the self-governments we are planning to establish in Voivodina. You might want me to give you exact amounts and percentages and compare these to the figures concerning the area where we live now, that is Voivodina, which was an autonomous territory for decades with its own constitution and quite a developed network of institutions for self-government. Obviously, in the present economic situation, it is very difficult to predict the exact amount of the GDP that can serve as a financial base of future autonomies. When we talk about autonomy we imagine a society with perfect conditions of free market economy where everybody will take part in production and management according to their ability and competence. But it will not be easy because in Yugoslavia the redistribution of revenues is too centralized, 76 per cent of the GDP is redistributed by the state. We know very well unfortunately that the territory of our would-be autonomy is discriminated against, especially because the sources of income mobilized by the population in Voivodina are overestimated: they simply take the income by cadastral acres as basis of assessment. It is 3.5-4 times higher than in similar territories in Serbia. This method of taxation is a perfect means to neutralize and disguise the differences of efficiency in different parts of the country by withdrawing larger amounts of money from more developed regions. That is why we try to propose more independence and authority for the future self-governments to control financial resources. Let me give an example of how the state withdraws incomes: while in Serbia the payable tax is between 18 and 50 per cent (Belgrade is an exception), in Zombor and Szabadka the same duty is 84 and 81 per cent respectively. When I speak about the neutralization of differences in efficiency I mean that here in Voivodina for example calculations in food production are made according to the fact that we can count on an average of 18 porkers per sow. The correspondent number in other areas in Serbia is 8.5, which makes a big difference as far as profit is concerned as well. To disguise and neutralize these differences the state "adjusts" tax requirements as we have seen above or overestimates the cadastral revenues, etc. thus gaining a higher percentage of tax from more developed regions and then it is called "fair" taxation. We do not think it is. We claim that this overcentralized system of redistribution should be restricted. I am not one hundred per cent sure that it is exactly those seven new self-governments that will bring Paradise for the Hungarian national minority, but we have a real chance to do better even with the present structure of ownership. We were extremely shocked by nationalization and we still are. Last year the Serbian Parliament renationalized 270, 000 acres of land which were actually public - and not state or cooperative assets. Since then it has been the government's right to appoint all the leaders and managers and to decide on the goods produced. The structure of ownership in Voivodina is very different from that of the other parts of Serbia. In Voivodina, in the territory of our would-be autonomy, 60% of the cultivated area is private, and 40% is state property. In other parts of Serbia 95% of the land is privately owned and only 5% is state property. We are not afraid of losing positions with the changes of economy and the ownership; we do not want privileges during the process of privatization, we only want a fair competition with equal conditions and opportunities. Nowadays it is not the case at all. For example in Serbia people can buy petrol for dinar, while in Voivodina we have to barter goods for gasoline. (1 litre petrol equals 7 kgs of wheat or 1 kg of heifer.) We have to go on fighting so that this highly developed region and its people should not be humiliated and exploited by forcing barter economy on it for example. Ultimately we aim at restricting and decentralizing the authority of a unitary state. That is why we believe that while fighting our ways towards autonomy we are building up the whole mechanism of the defence of minority rights. This fight involves the right to use our native language, to have our own educational institutions, etc. Since most of the inhabitants in the area live in villages, we must put special emphasis on working out mechanisms on how to develop and keep this culture and population alive. We cannot and we must not differentiate between a Hungarian and a Serbian farmer's pigs, but we need equal chances. As soon as we can enjoy equal chances in a free market economy, we will be able to create the necessary financial base to prosper and we will introduce a more fair system of redistribution. A person who is well-informed is a citizen, but the one who is not, is only a servant. Language and economy are two different things. On the one hand we fight for the laws of economy to prevail in the fields of economy, irrespective of the language, while on the other hand we demand equality for all the languages, may they use Cyrillic or Latin scripts.

Autonomy is often defined as a form of separatism. Hungarian readers had access to the book by a famous economist, Kosta Mihalovic, who is a member of the Serbian Academy of Science and who is a most important theorist and adviser of the government on economic issues. In his opinion autonomy equals separatism and as such, it is anti-socialist. He has his own arguments to prove that efforts for autonomy in economic life are antisocial as well. At least that was the reason when Voivodina was deprived of its old, traditional regional autonomy, and unfortunately the Serbian public believed this reasoning. We have long traditions of regional self-governments in Voivodina even from centuries ago. I do not say we will solve all our problems overnight if we have autonomy, but obviously we would be able to work out and realize a more fair and efficient system of production and distribution. We firmly believe that decentralization tendencies in economy help us realize our dreams and plans as far as autonomy is concerned as well.

The Unaccomplished State
Alpár Losoncz

Let me start with a short, general overview of the main aspects of the minority issue:

How does the forced historical development of a majority nation determine the concept of autonomy for a minority?

In what ways, if any, can the concept of autonomy influence the possible processes of democratization within the majority community?

Is it true, and how much, that the autonomy tendencies of a minority group always develop in the shadow of a majority community's struggles for establishing a nation state? What is more, is it sure that these tendencies develop in the shadow of the majority nation's tendencies at all?

I think the autonomy tendencies of any minority group, and thus those of the Hungarian national minority in Voivodina, in a way are reactions of defence. How should we judge a situation whose main element is defence? Can it be beneficial for the community? Are there any possibilities to translate this defensive position into a more creative offensive position? Is it possible that by thinking this issue over and over again we can force politicians in the East-Central European region to establish a new relationship between the idea of liberalism and that of collective rights.

I have already mentioned the phrase of "unaccomplished state," which I think is a basic category to understand the history of Yugoslavia from the very beginning. Yugoslavia has been struggling with the same problem and the frustrations resulting from it for a long time and its twentieth century history is actually nothing else but a series of different responses to this question. The notion of the "unaccomplished state" describes the period between the two world wars just as well as the Yugoslavia existing till the end of the eighties or the present day "third Yugoslavia." Despite all the political differences these states have something in common, namely that the actual form of government could always be kept only by force. And it is very likely that a system which can be kept only by force is counter-productive.

There is a metaphor often used in connection with the so-called post-communist regimes, and that is the metaphor of a "refrigerator". Communism functioned as a "refrigerator" all over East-Central Europe, which means it "deep-froze" and "preserved" all the important problems, contradictions and national conflicts typical of the region, without solving them. In the post-communist period this refrigerator stopped working and all the goods kept in it proved to be rotten. This metaphor is true for the present Yugoslavia as well. The problems that remained unsolved for two generations of governments are still problems, even if the conditions are very different now. The crucial problem in Yugoslavia is the relationship between the constitutional elements of the state. This question is not even asked in Yugoslavia. They do not even hint to the fact that there is a government which is not recognized by the International Community, that there is a set of institutions which is not able to stabilize its political practice.

I think we should make a difference between an ethnic- state and a nation-state. The former one is a depoliticized form of state, which means a community kept together by their common fate and history, their language and traditions. An ethnic-state is organized along the line of a politically structured set of institutions, while a nation-state is more than that and cannot be considered politically structured any longer. I think the whole twentieth century history of Yugoslavia can be described by this dual category. It is striking that any time a Southern Slavic nation - Serbian or Croatian - mentioned the problem of nation-state it always led to extreme violence. Unfortunately it is not very difficult to see continuity in the twentieth century history of Yugoslavia. This might sound strange since even five years ago Yugoslavia seemed to be a consolidated and stable state, where national conflicts were subdued and economic life was apparently more prosperous; in a word, it seemed to represent a higher level of development in every respect compared to other East-Central European countries. But now we have to admit that the (Bolshevik type) political leadership of the time could not solve a single national problem, or to be exact, they were experimenting with a very special solution, that is, they tried to form nation-type oligarchies. It is these oligarchies that are the participating leaders in the present war.

After the Second World War there appeared a special ideology in Yugoslavia, the so-called "Yugoslavianism", which claimed to be an above-national ideology. That was meant to serve as a means to prevent national conflicts; they expected all the nations, nationalities and national minorities to assert their national identities through this ideology. From the Hungarian national minority's point of view this above-all-nation ideology proved to be quite a tragic solution, because their assimilation after the Second World War reached an extremely high level. If I had to describe post-war Yugoslavia in a word, I would say it was the socialism of the threatened. There existed equality, but it was the equality created by threat. Obviously, when the real base of peaceful co-existence is fear of each other, it cannot be maintained for a long time. These are the circumstances in which different national minorities' autonomy conceptions came into life at the end of the eighties. If we think back on the dual category of ethnic-state and nation-state and the distinction I made between them, I suppose it is the nation-state which can be a real partner for a minority autonomy. Minority autonomies are real challenges for the nation-state. What does it involve to establish minority autonomies? Does it mean wedging a mini-state into the body of a nation-state and then these two more or less competent authorities will be rivals? It would be beneficial if the self-governments could show some self-restriction from the very beginning. It would require a certain amount of pluralism within the institutions of the minority itself. There is another form of pluralism that I would like to see realized in connection with minority autonomies. I think it is of crucial interest for any minority community to stimulate and support non-national civil organizations. Each of us here in this region has some experience of assimilation. The ideologized version of that non-national, above-all-nation approach had its very subtle means to manipulate all of us. Now we have to think of the self-defence mechanisms that can prevent us from being assimilated and help us communicate with the majority community while preserving our own identity at the same time. Usually we have negative criteria to describe this process. We generally claim that we have to trust in our identity lest we should lose it. It is really important but only as a starting point. In the course of inter-ethnic communication we need positive standards to make it possible for us to take part in the aspects of the everyday life we have to share with the majority society. It is the prime interest of any minority community to support different formations of civil society because just on their own they undoubtedly cannot compete successfully with the much stronger majority society. The majority community of a nation sate will always have means to force assimilation in one way or another. It is all very true of Serbia because owing to the war the Serbian state has such means that might result in large waves of migration.

Plans and Facts in Sub-Carpathia
Mihály Tóth

Attaining autonomy have a long tradition in Sub-Carpathia
and these tendencies have become stronger again. This process
started during the Gorbachev era when the empire was
collapsing and they tried to introduce a more liberal economic
policy, (perestroika) and that was the time when the state of the
Ukraine was established.

There are several plans in Sub-Carpathia concerning the
autonomy of the region:

1) establishing a special self-government covering the
whole territory of Sub-Carpathia as a county;

2) establishing an economic type of autonomy, a free
economic district, also encompassing the whole county;

3) setting up an administrative type of self-government,
guaranteeing territorial autonomy to the Hungarian national
minority in the region and

4) gaining cultural autonomy, the details of which I am not
going to discuss now.

The tendencies mentioned above are very different from any
other similar tendencies in other regions or countries in one
respect, namely that they have reached a certain level of
legality. As a Bill, it has been adopted at different levels of
local authorities (district and county levels) and has been

submitted to the Supreme Council and the Ukrainian Parliament.

The territorial autonomy in Sub-Carpathia can be approached from two different points of view: we can analyse the problem from the point of view of the different national minorities and we might have an economic approach.

On December 1, 1991 there was a general election in Sub-Carpathia concerning its territorial status and another one held in Beregszász County about forming a national district.

The overwhelming majority of the population - 78 per cent in the first case and 82 per cent in the second - supported autonomy and voted for establishing a national district, respectively. In spite of having no clear-cut principals laid down before the election, the results showed   a very unambiguous standpoint and a strong wish and demand for self-government. Although the native population in the county of Sub-Carpathia - irrespective of their national affiliation - lives in normal, consolidated and peaceful conditions without any national clashes or any traditional conflicts and confrontations from the past, the election has divided the natives, especially those of Slavic origin. But the degree of division has not reached a level that could have led to the secession of the Ukrainian and the Ruthenian population. Seeking new possibilities and separate, independent ways of development stems more from the historical past and the negative experiences after the Second World War. There is a strong feeling of threat on the part of the national minorities that Ukrainian nationalism might gain power again.

The Russian population settled in during the past decades and the Russian-oriented Greek Orthodox Church, which tried to do its best to gain more scope in the newly established state of the Ukraine, played an important part in helping to attain autonomy.

Unfortunately, not long after being submitted to Parliament, the self-government law was modified and the counties were deprived of the right to initiate bills. Nothing essential has happened in this case since then.

The draft bill uses the following arguments to support its reasoning:

Sub-Carpathia is situated in the middle of East-Central Europe in a relatively small area and it has four neighbouring countries.

The economic structure of the area can only develop in a normal way in the future if the district can integrate into international economic life.

Its ethnic and national minorities, the Hungarians, Romanians and Slovakians live in separate but homogeneous blocks close to the border of their nation-states. The fact that a part of the Ruthenian population refuses to identify themselves as Ukrainian makes the situation even more complicated.

According to the proposal Sub-Carpathia would be a specific administrative unit with a special right to autonomy and self-determination within the Ukraine and would be vested with special rights and licences to control economic life within the territory. All these rights would be confirmed by the Constitution and a particular law guaranteeing   territorial integrity for Sub-Carpathia as a part of the Ukraine as an unquestionable and unalterable right. Sub-Carpathia cannot be a part of any other state or administrative unit. The proposal demands that all the individual and collective human rights be guaranteed, as well as the right to establish autonomies based on different territorial, minority or personal rights. Separation of powers, namely the power of central administration and that of the counties is another issue of great importance. The draft

65

bill declares that all the minority languages are to be given equal status with the official language of the state and it is the inalienable right of the local authorities to determine the official language of the territory. It would also be the inalienable right of the local authorities to decide on further territorial divisions within a local area; different nationality and territorial autonomies would be established by plebiscites or referenda. The proposal demands that territorial authorities have an exclusive right equal to that of the state to control local resources. Territorial authorities should have the right to establish and modify their own statutes and work out and set up the institutions of self-government. The proposal would make it possible to establish administrative territorial units on a nationality and minority basis and adopt them as legal entities. According to the draft territorial authorities would have the right to organize and control referenda and censuses as well as to determine the status of economic and social unions and associations. Matters of dispute between the state and the self-governing body must be decided on in court.

The plans concerning the would-be territorial autonomy, based in Beregszász County, consist of three distinctive parts:

The first part concerns language. The proposal demands that within the territory of this special minority autonomy the Hungarian language should be granted equal status with the official language of the state and that the use of language as a right should be devolved to the local self-government.

The second part speaks about the possibilities of establishing and maintaining Hungarian cultural institutions in the area.

The third part deals with the economy and mainly concerns the idea of setting up an independent economic district.

There have been several versions of this plan since 1990, and it is practically the only proposal the central authorities in Kiev showed any willingness to deal with. Since all government offices competent in the issue had adopted the plan it was submitted to the Supreme Council whose committee discussed the matter at a plenary session. Although only a few votes short, unfortunately the proposal was refused.

Establishing an independent economic zone could be a solution to many problems. Owing to its special geographical features, the territory might be able to use its economic resources more efficiently as an independent unit and could find remedies to all those unresolved problems the previous regime had got stuck with. We should try and introduce market economy and work out all the infrastructural and financial background necessary for healthy regional relationships, transit traffic and trade as soon as possible.

The proposal that we all hope to be adopted sooner or later, plans to introduce special regulations concerning taxation, duties and other financial matters. Local authorities would have an exclusive right to control local resources. According to the plan the top managing organization responsible for all matters of the economy would be

independent of all state and local-government authorities. As far as duty regulations are concerned, the territory would be a duty-free area, which means that all the transit goods would be exempt from duty obligations. Taxes imposed on entrepreneurs have to comply with the present system of taxation, that is, it cannot be higher than fifty per cent. There should be a free exchange of currencies in the country as far as bank and other financial transactions are concerned. Entrepreneurs should be given special guarantees to compensate for their losses.

As we can see, these endeavours and tendencies are much too far-reaching and comprehensive to be simply called an issue of minority autonomy. Efforts to gain regional autonomy are a good example of this. Nevertheless, unless some form of international codification concerning autonomies has been laid down we cannot do too much, since all the aims mentioned above are interpreted as separatism in this region - and unfortunately certain political leaders in Kiev are not free from all these biases either.

The Region of the Ukraine - the Autonomy of Crimea

István Ijjártó

We have known about several plans concerning the autonomy of Sub-Carpathia in the twentieth century. It all started in 1918, during the time of the newly established Hungarian Republic, when in compliance with the so-called X People's Act, the Károlyi government gave autonomy to the region of Ruszka-krajina, which would have guaranteed national autonomy for the Ruthenians in the North-Eastern part of the region. As a result of later events, partly because in the meantime Czechoslovakian and Romanian armies intervened in the region, the territory became part of Czechoslovakia in accordance with the Trianon Treaty. Although there had been an earlier political agreement between the members of the Ruthenian emigration of the time and the Czechoslovakian government, it was not in effect till the events in Munich. Then there was a very short period again when the Czechoslovakian government more or less already in power gave autonomy to the Ruthenian minority. Meanwhile, those territories where the inhabitants were Hungarian became a part of Hungary again. The rest of the area had become an Ukrainian-oriented state, called Carpathian Ukraine. In 1939 Hungarian authorities reintroduced Hungarian administration into the whole area of Sub-Carpathia. During the long period of Soviet superiority any possibility of autonomy was out of the question, of course. In spite of all the demands for autonomy, Sub-Carpathia was integrated into the then Ukrainian-Soviet Socialist Republic as a common administrative unit. The constant movement of this territory between the peripheries of the East and the West, which was mainly due to the special characteristics of the local Slavic inhabitants, definitely helped a lot to strengthen a kind of separatism and the idea of independence and self-government.

The next important turning point was the collapse of the Soviet Union. The decisive referendum was held on December 1, 1991 and its main concern for the Ukrainians was the creation of their nationhood. At the same time there was another referendum in the whole territory of Sub-Carpathia and in Beregszász County about forming an autonomous national district. The result and the validity of this latter election is unquestionable. As soon as we have doubts about it, we question the validity and the legality of the whole referendum that legitimized the independence of the Ukraine. In spite of this, I think we cannot avoid examining the touchy question of whether the Ukraine can be considered to be united - not in an administrative sense of course. Irrespective of the whole problem of Sub-Carpathia, the question is very important, because during its long history the territory of the present Ukraine belonged to different authorities. The other thing that makes the whole problem even more complicated is that it gained new territories - mainly in the west - which traditionally did not belong to the Ukraine and were especially the results of Russian expansion. The problems mentioned above have a very strong influence on the decision-makers' attitude and their fears and worries about the future of the Ukraine. If we take a closer look of the territory, we can see three different regions, a western, an eastern and a southern part. The West-Ukraine traditionally lived under Polish authority and was Greek-Catholic, which was a very important characteristic. On the contrary, the East-Ukraine was Russian-oriented and most of the time lived under the authority of the Russian Empire and the inhabitants, most of whom were Russians, belonged to the Greek Orthodox Church. The South-Ukraine was a special bumper area with a lot of people resettled during the Russian Empire. The Polish Kingdom, the Russian Empire and the Tartars of Crimea had long fights for the territory, which is well reflected in the ethnic complexity of the area and which makes it a bit different from the other two parts.

The political group which most unambiguously represents the interests of the Ukrainian nationhood and identity has a West-Ukrainian background and is concentrated in the area of the former so-called Galitia. I do not mean to dispute the true loyalty to the state of the Ukrainians and non-Ukrainians living in the eastern part of the country, but the demand for a Ukrainian nationhood has always been stronger and more explicit here, than anywhere else. The eastern parts seem to be less definite in this respect, partly because of the fact that they belonged to the Russian Empire, then to the Soviet Union for a long time and partly because they have a considerably large community of Russian origin.

When we speak about the Ukraine today, we must not forget about the events in Crimea. Crimea plays a very important part in our discussion, because the Republic of Crimea is the only legitimate regional autonomy with its own administrative authorities already existing and working in the Ukrainian region. Parallel to the events in Sub-Carpathia - though in many respects in a very different way - Crimea as well succeeded in achieving a kind of regional autonomy. Although there are a lot of differences between these two attempts, we must be careful not to overestimate and overemphasize the exclusively Russian characteristics of this movement and attribute its success only to its Russian background. It is true, of course, that the Russian population has an emphatic role in

71

the region - they are the largest in number (12.5 million, which means 25 % of the whole population in the Ukraine) - and it has its effect on political life as well, which might have added a lot to the success of the Crimeans. But as Mihály Tóth has mentioned before, it was not the only factor that led to victory.

Crimea became an administrative unit of the Ukraine in the 1850s, so in a way it is a strong symbol of successful Russian expansions during the Czarist era. On the other hand, we must not forget about the fact, that Crimea played an important economic and political role for the Russian nomenclature during the Communist regime as well. It was the scene of numerous important political meetings or that of the fall of prominent politicians, etc. Thus, when in the summer of 1992 the Crimeans decided to take a radical step and under the leadership of the so-called republic movement they were on the verge of demanding a referendum in August and claim for secession, all these factors must have influenced the process beneficially and helped them to succeed, including the inertia of the government in Kiev, which though reluctantly agreed to give autonomy to Crimea - but only within the Ukraine. With the exception of Sub-Carpathia there is no other example in the Ukraine of attempts to gain regional autonomy, though there are some signs of similar movements attempting to attain a kind of national and cultural autonomy in the vicinity of Odessa.

This leads us to the following question: what is the legal situation like in the Ukraine at present? What are the possibilities and chances for asserting national identities and minority rights? How can the different autonomy conceptions be put into practice - if they can?

The most important problem is that the new state does not have a constitution. The constitution in force was born in 1977, during the Soviet era. The Ukrainian Parliament has been performing some constitutional jobs, but up till now without any results. They have not had too many Bills as far as regional autonomy is concerned. With the exception of Crimea there are no other final versions of autonomy known. This makes it more difficult to try and incorporate national and minority rights in the constitution as well.

Nevertheless, it does not mean there are no legal results at all. One of them is for example the language act of the Ukrainian Socialist Republic, which was born within the framework of the previous Soviet regime and which together with similar language acts of other republics represents the first steps of a process towards national sovereignty. These acts were primarily aimed at restricting the official usage of Russian but did not mean too much restriction as far as different minority languages were concerned.

The other important legal result, which is quite exceptional in the region, is the national minority law. If we examine it thoroughly, we can find a lot of elements of the most important international documents on the issue, namely those of the UN, the European Security and Coordinating Assembly and the Council of Europe. Although it is not as elaborate as the minority law adopted by the Hungarian Parliament, which carefully covers a wide range of problems, it gives a lot of possibilities for the minorities to use their rights in a lot of issues, not only in language. It is true that it does not mention regional autonomy, but it provides good possibilities for cultural autonomy. There was a kind of relationship between Hungary and the Ukraine in this question during the preliminary work on the bill: they signed an agreement called Declaration on the Rights of National Minorities in 1991. One of the sources of this agreement was the Copenhagen document of the ESCA, a lot of points of which were well adapted.

Nevertheless, I would like the emphasise again, there is no mention about regional autonomy in this law.

To summarize: as we can see, there are two possible approaches of examining the events today: one from the point of view of Sub-Carpathia and another one from that of Kiev. The stake for Kiev - and I do not think I am exaggerating - is the survival of its statehood and the existence of the state in the long run might depend on its territorial status. There is a fact which was given less publicity during the election campaigns, which also ended on December 1, namely that the main opposition movement, the RUH, which is deeply rooted in Ukrainian traditions, had a proposal on federalism. After the elections this proposal remained unheard of for a while because it did not fit into the political plans and ideas of the new political elite. Recently these proposals have been taken up again and there have been talks about a kind of federal system, in which all of the regions would enjoy more or less the same rights as the Republic of Crimea does now and Crimea would get more authority.

In my opinion, Sub-Carpathia will have to face two important challenges in the near future: can it keep up the idea of autonomy till the Ukrainian state consolidates itself and there might be some possibilities to realize this idea? Or, if this hope fails, how will the future form of federalism integrate Sub-Carpathia as an administrative unit, and how will it influence the history of the region and the people' s life there?

The Crisis in the Ukraine
Tamás Réti

It is a well-known fact that the Ukraine is struggling with a serious economic crises, which is probably one of the most serious ones among the former republics of the Soviet Union. The country has experienced a sharp fall of the GDP, which means that the economy has suffered such an extreme "contraction" for the last few years that is unusual even in this region. The Ukraine has by far the highest consumer price index among the former republics of the Soviet Union and the inflation rate is rocketing up much faster than in Russia or any other states of the former Soviet Union. As a result, the economic position of the Ukraine is getting worse and worse compared to that of Russia. Let me mention only one symptom, namely the appalling devaluation of the Ukrainian currency-substitute in relation to the ruble. Considering the Russian-Ukrainian economic relations, the Ukraine tends to be more and more dependent on Russian economy and bilateral trade relationships, which have always been very distorted and asymmetric, have not changed either, or if they have, even for the worse. Experts usually emphasise two things: first, Ukrainian economy is extremely dependent on Russian fuel. They succeeded in diversifying their buying a bit, but their demands for oil and natural gas are basically met by Russia. The volume of fuel Russia sends to the Ukraine is steadily decreasing and this tendency can be expected to be stronger in the future. At the same time, Russia is trying to bring its prices closer to the world market prices and get more for its fuel - and in hard currency, if it is possible. If we examine the 1992 balance of trade regarding Russia and the Ukraine, we can see that the latter had a trade deficit equal to 6.6 per cent of the GDP and this ratio was even worse for 1993. The country is in big financial troubles, on the verge of insolvency and totally unable to pay its bills. As a result, in the summer of 1993 Russia cancelled its oil import to the Ukraine. Ukrainian industry does not have enough capacity to produce consumer goods for export and the country cannot discharge its export liabilities determined in different bilateral trade agreements and in spite of all the contracts it had to stop taking part in different common investments. Russian raw material bills remain unpaid in an increasing number and it is quite understandable that Russia is trying to decrease or cease its exports and making the conditions more and more difficult. The Ukrainian leadership would have liked to believe that they would be supplied with abundant quantities of Russian oil and natural gas at a very good price and was surprised to realize it was not so and there was a radical change. They would have liked to take advantage of the fact that 95 per cent of Russian deliveries go through their territory and claimed an unrealistically high price for transit traffic, which went well beyond the highest world market prices. But their efforts did not bring them any results and it left them in a much worse bargaining position.

The Russian economic policy has two choices in relation with the Ukraine: first, it might be ready to take political aspects into consideration and bear more unfavourable conditions and prices in trade with the Ukraine, including a rescheduling of Ukrainian debts. The other possibility is to trade on normal terms, which would mean a much more unfavorable, almost impossible position for the Ukraine. What can the Ukraine do in such difficult circumstances, how can it discharge its debts with such a serious foreign trade deficit as far as Russia is concerned? The word is, the Ukraine is trying to offer capital assets to counterbalance its deficit. It uses a part of the country's national wealth to discharge its debts, for instance it is said to have offered some gas-distributing equipment to some Russian gas producing companies. The question is, how far Russia is ready to go to take responsibility for its former republics and take steps to prevent inter-republic trade from collapsing? It is a well-known fact that the Russian national bank used to provide huge amounts of credit to keep up this trade and this unbelievable amount of credit was in large part responsible for the Russian hyperinflation.

Ukrainian leadership should do much more in such a situation. They should try and establish favourable conditions for market economy as soon as possible, they should stimulate export, restructure the industry, relieve their dependence on Russia and most of all, they should take urgent steps to stabilize the country by decreasing the extremely high inflation. Taken the present situation there seems to be very little chance of their being able to take such steps. At present there are no concrete plans to struggle and try to beat inflation. Let me give an example: in 1993 the Ukrainian economic policy ploughed huge amounts of credit into agriculture, which increased the already high inflation to an extremely high degree. Since the Ukrainian economic policy does not seem to have any means or possibilities to stabilize the country and introduce market economy in the near future and since the economic circumstances are quite chaotic they are very likely to resort to a non-market type of means alien to market economy again, such as centralization and state intervention. There are some elements in the central redistribution of goods reintroduced into the economy again, there are some steps taken backwards in the liberalization of foreign trade and as a result of an artificial price control the state can offer the companies an extremely low price

77

for the compulsory quota of their export incomes. This administrative, non-market type of leadership cannot do any good to the economy, just the opposite: instead of improving the economic situation it probably deepens the crisis and deteriorates the country's conditions. I completely understand Sub-Carpathia when it claims to have a special economic belt within the Ukraine. This kind of decentralization would be desirable and beneficial of course, but I do not think the phrase "special autonomous belt" is the best term to describe their demands and it has some political overtones, which I do not consider appropriate either. It is simply economic decentralization. Decentralization has its own dangers of course. When central authorities devolve a part of economic responsibilities on local authorities, it is unavoidable that these local administrative units gain more economic power as a result. In this case it is a real danger that the bureaucratic, administrative methods typical of the central powers will gain more ground at local levels as well.

It is not a surprise that the Ukrainian leadership interprets its economic difficulties and the increase of Russian dominance as a restriction of its sovereignty. And basically they are right. Being in such a vulnerable situation I do not think the Ukrainian leadership could be open to hail the idea of economic decentralization and let any region gain more authorities. From pure economic reasons it would be logical to try and get as far as possible from the sinking ship of the Ukrainian economy and board our own lifeboats. But there is still the question whether it is possible at all to get out of the whirlpool of this big ship and if so, is it possible to row these boats at a higher speed than the ship sails.

The Autonomy Conceptions of the
Slovakian Liberals
László Ollos

In 1989, and later when we were working out our conceptions on autonomy, the most important principle we tried to keep in mind was that our self-government must not have a destabilizing effect on the developing bourgeois democracy in Czechoslovakia. Minority autonomy must not restrain any democratic tendencies in the country as a whole. On the contrary, we must support all the efforts to enhance the democratization and modernization of all institutions especially those that can help us develop the institutions of national autonomies and the ones that might be in close relations with the new institutions of these autonomies. Minority autonomies must not exert a destabilizing effect on the country, because it weakens democracy, which can endanger autonomies themselves, since democracy is an indispensable precondition for their existence and efficient working.

The other important criterion we had to take into account was that any existing form of minority autonomy should be able to meet all the demands of a given community - in our case those of the Hungarian national minority in Czechoslovakia - especially those that are in connection with their national identity. Minority autonomies should be flexible enough to be able to present and represent all the important cultural, educational, linguistic, economic and other interests of a minority community in a successful and efficient way in the whole of a given country.

The third principle is that the concept of autonomy should not mainly function as an emotional political program which stirs up national feelings, but that it should rather be a workable plan. That is, it must not contain contradictory and overlapping elements; elements that are in contradiction with the working mechanisms of an existing state or that might result in situations where decision-making can be made very difficult because of the presence of overlapping fields. This plan - if it really wants to be feasible - should be based on the special characteristics of the given nation, which means in our case for example that these plans should take all the cultural, economic, geographical and other characteristics of the Hungarian national minority in Slovakia into consideration.

The group I was lucky to work with on the topic of Hungarian minority autonomy in Slovakia tried to work out a concept of autonomy which had four important elements.

The first element is that of educational and cultural autonomy. It requires a set of institutions with a management elected in a free and democratic way. Naturally, it has an executive apparatus and a budget and is vested with all the rights to control all the cultural and educational institutions of the Hungarian minority in Slovakia, that is, it is authorized to establish or close down schools, different cultural institutions, etc. Its authority can be restricted only in one respect. Minority public schools cannot have a curriculum which is in sharp contradiction with the basic curriculum used nationwide, which means for example that mathematics cannot be taught in minority schools in a totally different way than in all the other schools in the country. The basic elements of the minority's cultural and educational autonomy must fit somehow into the main tendencies and institutional system of the majority society, but at the same time, all the important national characteristics of the minority must be asserted and reflected in these institutions.

The second element concerns the right to use the native language. In our opinion, it must be an individual human right, so it is not exactly a matter of autonomy. The best solution in this respect would be to establish a bilingual zone in Slovakia, that is, in territories where there is a large Hungarian community, both Slovakian and Hungarian must be official languages. This solution would stop the futile debate on what per cent is enough to entitle a citizen to use his or her native language in justice and administration and other official matters. There are some good examples working in Europe and we do not think it would require special, impracticable measures in administration. In that case, even those Hungarians who live in minority in a special settlement would not be deprived of the right to use their native language. Bilingualism would guarantee the same rights for the Slovakians of course, that is they would be entitled to use their native language in the future as well, even in those settlements and regions where they are in minority.

The third important element of autonomy is regionalism. In our interpretation regionalism means a free association of settlements, a means to give voice to our common local interests. In the present constitution of Slovakia there is only one sentence which mentions the right to establish regions but it does not specify their authority or their structural characteristics, etc. In spite of this, regionalism is prospering in Slovakia nowadays, including areas with mixed population and regions where either the Hungarians or the Slovakians are in the majority. These regions are organized - almost without any exception - according to economic interests. This system works exceptionally well and efficiently, especially in areas where the population is mixed, common interests might even bring people of different origin closer together. Our constitution,

81

similar to that of several West European nations' should determine all the authorities every single region can demand if they wish to and which can be laid down in their regional statutes and in their fundamental rules. The inner structure of a region would be based on democracy as well (with inside elections, for example). Regionalism, of course, is in close connection with decentralization and devolution of central authorities. The aim is to devolve as many authorities on local and regional levels as possible, including the matters of tourism, road network, forestry and water works, agriculture, some aspects of cultural and educational life and most of the rights in connection with the basic development of the region.

The fourth element, which - although, it is not a par excellence autonomy question again - belongs to the core of the problem, is the question of medium level units of administration. It would be essential that medium level administration (the district and the zone level) be built up more or less according to the ethnic composition of a region. Naturally, this kind of administration is an organic part of the state administration and as such it is not actually a part of autonomy.

The kind of autonomy analysed above does not make it possible to centralize power at the level of minority autonomies. The institutions of cultural and educational autonomy are competent only in local issues. On the other hand, this concept of autonomy could prevent a large number of Hungarians in Slovakia from being deprived of the advantages of autonomy. A considerable part of the Hungarian national minority in Slovakia lives in a strip along the Hungarian-Slovakian border, but this strip is not continuous. Actually the Hungarian population is concentrated in three different areas, which are not really connected administratively. I would hasten to add another fact, namely that almost one third of the Hungarian national minority in Slovakia lives in a minority even within their own settlements. Most of the cities along the border or close to the border live under Slovakian majority, so city dwellers are not in a a better position at all. When planning a future autonomy, we have to find a solution which makes it possible to assert and represent the common cultural and educational interests in spite of all these difficulties stemming from scatteredness. We need a system that does not deprive anybody of his or her rights. That is why the solution mentioned above seems to be appropriate. Let me give an example: it is indeed possible that a settlement belongs to different region. The borders cannot be fixed and closed they have to be adjusted according to local and regional interests. Most of the elements of this system can fit organically into the whole process of democratization, since it is not a mere minority interest to devolve authorities to local and regional governments. It is in the interest of the whole country as well to lay down clear-cut, well-defined rules to regulate how different minority communities can use their own language in administration, and to establish a new administrative power at regional level in accordance with local and regional interests.

Christian Democrats on Autonomy
János Fóti

In Slovakia, the concept of autonomy has been worked out by two minority groups, the Hungarian Christian Democratic Movement of Slovakia and the Political Movement for Coexistence. After the changing of the regime the situation in Slovakia was very similar to that of the other East-Central European countries. Our illusions convinced us that after the fall of the dictatorships all our economic, social and minority problems would be solved overnight. Instead, we have deteriorating economies and increasing nationalism. In our country we experience both in an extreme way, mainly because of the separation of the two parts of the country.

Slovakia has become an independent nation as a result of a delayed development, so it is not a surprise that those in power are thinking in terms of a nation-state. It is not an accident that the constitution of Slovakia does not say: "We, the citizens of Slovakia" but it starts instead with the following words: "We, the Slovakian nation" - in spite of the fact that 15 per cent of the population is not of Slovakian origin. Considering the factors that help to preserve a nation's identity, we can find the following things in Slovakia: minorities have restricted rights to use their national language, there is a kind of discriminative law in force in this respect; the educational system is centralized. During the period of dictatorship there was a Hungarian Department at the Ministry of Education, which was responsible for the Hungarian schools, but sadly we no longer have it. We have to face the danger of having alternative education introduced in our schools, which would mean that only Hungarian language, literature and history could be taught in Hungarian. Hungarian teachers' training colleges will be closed down, because though Act 34 of the Slovakian Constitution guarantees all minorities the right to get proper education in their own language, In Nyitra, for example, Hungarian education is permitted only in the first four classes of primary school.

In 1960 there was a "territorial arrangement" in Slovakia. Whereas before this arrangement there used to be nine districts where Hungarians lived as the majority, as a result of these measures there remained only two, Dunaszerdahely and Kom_rom. As a result of a new territorial arrangement in the pipeline, which would divide the country in a North-South direction, there might not be any Hungarian majority county or district left in Slovakia. No wonder the Hungarian autonomy proposals have been refused saying that it was no longer a feasible plan with 1.2 million Slovakians living in the territory. No hint is made, of course, about the fact that we are in this situation only because of the territorial arrangements.

Another "trick" often used today to distort facts is that they always speak about "mixed areas" and never a mention is made about Hungarian inhabited areas. Since there are national majorities in every single district - if not Hungarians, Romanians or gypsies at least - all the territory of Slovakia can be considered to be a "mixed area". It is enough just to mention the word "autonomy" and authorities suspect separatism and an attack against the integrity of the country. At the same time, unfortunately, common Slovakian citizens are suspicious and hostile as well.

Nowadays democracy is a privilege of the majority in Slovakia and there is no political will to solve even the basic problems of minority rights, let alone autonomy.

Administrative Measures Proposed by the Political Movement for Coexistence
Piroska Gyuricsek

There are 523 villages altogether is Slovakia where we can find Hungarian inhabitants. In 429 cases Hungarians are in an absolute majority, which means their ratio is above 50 per cent. There are 8 more villages where they are in a relative majority. We speak about a relative majority when there are several different ethnic communities in a settlement and none of them are in an absolute majority. As far as the eight villages mentioned above are concerned, the ratio of the Hungarian inhabitants is 47 per cent there. I deny the proposition therefore, that there are no cities with Hungarian majority at all. It is true there are not too many, but in Dunaszerdahely and Somorja, for example, their ratio is around 80 per cent. In Nagymegyer (Csallóköz) the ratio of the Hungarian nationality is very high, 97-98 per cent. We all know the reason why towns and cities have such low ratios; the previous regimes tried to solve the minority issue by industrializing Hungarian areas and settling Slovakians there. That is why we have Slovakians in a majority in places like Nyitra for example. But even Nyitra is surrounded by villages with a definite Hungarian majority and I am sure that the name of Gerencsér, for example, sounds familiar to all those who know Hungarian folk songs. This case is a typical example of geographically scattered and interspersed areas. The conception of autonomy in the Movement for Coexistence is based on the postulate that there is a definite strip in the south of the country inhabited mostly by Hungarians. There is only one clear break in this strip, which is unambiguously the result of the territorial and settlement policies of the previous regimes. If we compare present maps with those from 1910, the differences are striking. Considering all these facts, we think in the terms of territorial autonomy and are proposing to establish small nationality districts in the area. Presumably the fact that this strip is very long cannot be an obstacle to territorial autonomy, since there are examples of similar administration units in Burgenland for example. That is why the Movement for Coexistence - unlike the Hungarian Bourgeois Party for example - considers territorial autonomy as a key to the problem and wishes to follow the example of the South Tyrol or Catalania. We do not believe cultural autonomy alone can bring a final, reassuring solution. The strip I mentioned before could be established using the previous district system as a base. In case of a territorial system - and there are already plans for such a system - we could have two Hungarian provinces. The latest plans refer to a county or regional system. In that case we could count on three or four counties. Actually, the laws on self-governments make it possible for settlements to unite and form a common administrative unit. We already have such units, or regions as legal entities in Csallóköz and Bodrogköz, which are actually associations of towns and villages.

A Debate with Empathy
Rudolf Chmel

My present situation is a bit strange for me, because here and now I am supposed to represent an opinion that at home I would not be able to give voice to; that is, the opinion of a Slovakian nationalist. For the sake of the debate I will try to show empathy in my approach. One thing is certain; in the fifties, sixties and seventies there was always unity and agreement in Slovakia as far as Hungarian-Slovakian relations were concerned, and there is still unity and agreement on the Slovakian side. Emigrants, communists, dissidents, democrats - almost everybody agreed on the so-called Hungarian question. Nothing has changed in this respect so far, not even in the past few years or months. The new independent state of Slovakia was not prepared for the changes in any respect - neither in a psychological nor in a practical sense, let alone the legal consequences - and could not offer any new solution to the minority issue. Unfortunately, it is now a fact. When a Slovakian politician (irrespective of his or her political beliefs and affiliations) hears the word "autonomy" he or she automatically suspects a source of danger. In a way this fear is understandable, since there is a lot of confusion and misunderstanding around the concept itself even in the literature.

I have consulted some textbooks on the legal aspects of the problem and I was compelled to realize that even in the thirties - let alone the following communist era - they could not distinguish between the concepts of autonomy and self-government. Not long ago there was a television programme in the course of which I had the opportunity to ask Miklós Duray about autonomy. When I asked him to define the concept of autonomy he answered it was self-government. When I asked him whether he supported autonomy or not, he answered yes, he was a fervent supporter of the idea of self-government and a fervent supporter of autonomy. This terminological confusion has fatal consequences. We cannot solve this problem because for Slovakian politicians and for the public as well autonomy equals territorial autonomy. It causes a lot of dangerous problems and misunderstanding in both home and foreign affairs. Autonomy - irrespective of its concrete forms - is certainly a sign of political decentralization. This is an easy question from a theoretical point of view, but unfortunately reality makes this problem much more complicated. I am deeply sorry but I have to ask everybody here: what kind of autonomy do you have in mind when you speak about autonomy - cultural, educational or territorial autonomy? If they are talking about territorial autonomy in the south of Slovakia for example, they should be more exact about the form of autonomy they would have liked to achieve when they refer to the political situation in 1910, when there was, in my opinion, an aggressive nationalistic tendency on the side of the Hungarians. These historical prejudices are still very strong and cannot be ignored completely. If we refer back to the situation during the last century or the Trianon Treaty and the demographic changes, we get tangled up in an infinite debate and can never find a solution.

We have to consider the present demographical situation as a fact: there are about 900,000 people of Slovakian origin living in the south of the country. We have to find political and not historical solutions and it is very difficult of course because both sides are quite steadfast in their stands. I have to take the liberty to confront not only the Slovakian government and the

Slovakian nationalists but also the Hungarian politicians because I have some experience of their policies as well. The question of borders is another sore issue and it is not only a matter of minority but of international importance. It would be essential to find a solution that could be reassuring for both sides. I do not think we should treat the minority issue and the border issue as one single question, but unfortunately they cannot be completely separated. If we could solve the border issue in a reassuring way, in accordance with the international agreements in force, I am sure we could have greater prospects of finding a better solution in the minority issue as well.

Minorities in Lithuania
Halina Kobeskaite

Act 29 of the Lithuanian Constitution makes it possible for everybody to belong to a national minority. Acts 1, 2 and 8 of the Minority Law consider the same problem. It is laid down very clearly in Act 2 that all minority groups have the right to represent themselves at all levels of administration, which must be the result of general, equal and direct elections and that any member of a minority community can be a candidate for any post in state and government administration, and they can apply for any job at any company, institution or organization. The Minority Law admits it is a duty of the state to guarantee equal political, economic, social and human rights for all citizens. Besides this, the state is obliged to prevent all racial, national or linguistic discrimination and to punish any signs of them. It is also said in the same law that it is forbidden to force anybody to prove his or her national identity against their will.

By establishing the Institution of Citizenship every single citizen - Lithuanian or non-Lithuanian - is said to be equal by law. The new law of citizenship is clear evidence of the Lithuanian authorities' desire to guarantee equal rights to minorities and consider them as non-alienable members of society. The so-called "zero-version" reinforces the same idea, saying that all citizens of Lithuania, irrespective of their origin, can attain citizenship. The same idea can be found in the constitution as well. At present 87 per cent of the inhabitants are Lithuanian citizens.

The criteria for gaining Lithuanian citizenship have not changed in the middle of the country for a long time: they are practically the same as they were before the Second World War.

The south-eastern part of the country is very different, having been much more sovietized.

Minority issues often play an important role in political games. It is especially true for the eastern part of the country. There have been several occasions when they tried to justify cases of discrimination. Fortunately they have always failed to do so. Nevertheless, we have to expect similar cases in the future as well, especially for political reasons, because unfortunately minority issues can always be manipulated by politicians.

Allow me to continue with another legal aspect of the minority issue, that is, let me refer to the principle that all citizens are equal by law. This law declares that every citizen has equal rights to take part in the economic, social, political and cultural life of society. The political and other organizations of different national minorities can have a seat in Parliament even below the required four per cent limit. As a consequence, the Polish Alliance of Lithuania could get two seats in Parliament. This act is of crucial importance, because it is the only law that guarantees collective rights to national minorities - the other acts concern individual rights. In the course of the 1933 Parliamentary elections the people of Lithuania had the opportunity to elect three "extra" MPs. At present there is a Polish fraction in Parliament and other nationalities have Parliamentary representatives as well, but they are elected on the "usual" party lists. After the regional council elections in Vilnius we established a self-government, most of the members of which are of Polish origin. As we know, 64 per cent of the inhabitants are of Polish origin in this region. Polish people have representatives in other regions, where their ratio is between 16 and 30 per cent.

I suppose it is quite clear from my lecture that at present the question of minority autonomy is not an issue in Parliament or in the government, but it is not a matter of discussion for the Polish Alliance of Lithuania or the Polish fraction in Parliament either.

Local self-governments in Lithuania have been organized according to the national system of administration. They have comprehensive authority and a large scope of autonomy in decision making. But it is not a matter of national minority at all. I think we have to be careful to make a distinction between the two issues. In my opinion, in most post-communist regimes minority and nationality issues can be best solved by guaranteeing individual autonomy to everybody. In this period of transition the main concern of these countries should be to discharge all the creative energies in individuals and to assure them equal chances to realize their individuality. It should be left to the individual to decide whether he or she wishes to belong to a national minority or not; it is none of the state's business. What the state must do is to make sure that all the vital conditions and rights should be provided for the minority communities to prosper. The state has numerous means to perform this duty: it can make special legal provisions and take special measures to enforce them. In my opinion, citizenship is the only way for the individuals to get integrated in the general processes of the state. In Lithuania, for example, most private properties are owned by Russians. Nevertheless, I do not think matters of business life or taxation should be connected with minority issues or the problems of national identity. I do not consider it wise to "lead" the minority card in the field of economics or politics.

When discussing minority rights we also have to mention duties. Firstly, there are duties that should be fulfilled for the state we are living in and secondly, we have duties as citizens.

Social duties apply to everybody, I assume, irrespective of national affiliations; that is members of a national minority community cannot have privileges in this respect, but they must not have extra burdens either. All the members of a minority community are supposed to speak the official language of the given state; it is not only one of the most important duties, but also a means to their self-accomplishment. In Lithuania - like in any other previously occupied territory - we have to face a very unusual and complicated question. It is undoubtedly necessary for everybody to speak the language of the state and country they live in. Nowadays the situation is getting better: everybody can decide whether they stay where they live or settle somewhere else. In a word, things are happening spontaneously. In Western societies national minorities also speak the official language of the country where they live, but the state is obliged to guarantee all the institutional conditions that make it possible for these communities to learn and use their own languages so that they can foster their cultural roots and traditions and assert their national identities. In our country both the official and the minority languages are taught.

It is of vital importance here in the East-Central European region to make it possible for all minority groups to foster their own cultural traditions and values and assert their own national identities and affiliations, but at the same time every single citizen must be assured the right to integrate into the political, cultural and social life of the given country.

National Minorities in Bulgaria
Krassimir Kanev

According to the latest census of December 1992, in Bulgaria there are 822,000 Turks, 288,000 Gypsies, 65,000 Bulgarian-speaking Muslims, 25,000 Armenians and several other smaller nationalities, such as Tartars, Gagauzes, Russians, Jews and 7,000 Macedonians. The data concerning the gypsy population must be taken with certain reservations, because an estimated fifty per cent must have identified themselves as Bulgarians and another part as Turks. Most of the Macedonians cannot have admitted their nationality either. The explanation must be found in the negative, discriminative bahaviour on the side of both the central and the local authorities.

During the previous political regime there were two serious campaigns against the Turks and the Muslims in Bulgaria, aiming to assimilate them, one at the beginning of the 1970s, and the other in the middle of the 1980s. In 1989 there was a huge flood of Turkish emigration. Besides that, another group of Turks have left the country for Turkey for economic reasons.

In theory, autonomy can be a solution, especially when a minority population is sufficiently numerous and concentrated and is in a better economic position than the majority nationality. I think it is important to make a distinction between the two basic forms of autonomy, namely between territorial and cultural autonomy. In my opinion, it is not always necessary to have them both simultaneously. I mean, territorial autonomy does not always imply cultural autonomy.

Let me give an example from Bulgaria to support my statement. Let's examine how much the concept of territorial autonomy can be applied to the Turkish nationality in Bulgaria. At present there are very few settlements where the Turks are in a majority. This situation is the result of a long process including huge floods of emigration for economic reasons (like the one in 1992) and partly for political reasons, because for the past few decades there has been quite a strong discriminative policy against them on the side of the central powers. Most of the Turks live in the economically underdeveloped mountainous areas in Bulgaria. As a result, these administrative units where there is a relatively substantial Turkish population do not really fight for territorial autonomy. Most of them need to be subsidized in all fields of life, including economic infrastructure, social benefits and education.

There is a strong feeling of fear among the Turkish population that, provided the Bulgarian national community gets stronger and larger in number in their regions, they will be exposed to more discrimination and they will be deprived of even more human rights.

In 1992 there was a nation-wide survey in Bulgaria examining the inhabitants' attitude towards national minorities. According to the results, Bulgarians living in a majority but mingled with different minority groups, are more hostile in their attitude towards national minorities than the national average. In 1991, when the teaching of the Turkish language was introduced, nationalist groups did not agree with it, saying the decision should have been made at a local level. But in that case there would not have been any decision. The truth is that the Turkish language was broadly introduced only when the central authorities took the initiative. Many are afraid that if self-governments get stronger, they will stimulate a kind of inner emigration so as to establish ethnically pure regions. Instead of mixed regions there would be a pure Turkish and a pure Bulgarian region for example. In the case of such a development the basic minority rights of the Turkish community would not be respected.

Nowadays the most difficult case of the minority issue in Bulgaria is that of the Gypsies. In their case the principles of territorial autonomy is totally out of the question because they live geographically scattered and interspersed. Allow me to make a remark before I go on: according to the law in Bulgaria each minority group is entitled to equal treatment and rights. The Bulgarian law does not make any distinction between a national or an ethnic minority, all the minority groups are referred to as ethnic. When the Turkish language was introduced into the country, they started to teach the Gypsy language as well. Since last year an estimated 30,000-40,000 Gypsy children have been able to get education in their own language. These possibilities are of course assured to other national minorities as well, such as the Armenians and the Jews, who can benefit from this possibility after normal school hours. The state gives substantial financial help for this.

I would like to emphasize the role of the government in the defence of individual human rights as well, especially in the case of the Gypsies. The Gypsies' human rights are usually offended at local levels and are only - if ever - defended at a central level.

In theory, I am not against autonomy as a kind of solution. It can be used in a lot of cases. But at the same time we always have to consider the responsibilities and the functions of the government as well. We must keep in mind that even autonomy cannot be an impeccable solution, for it also has its negative effects.

Gypsies in Bulgaria
Rumian Russinov

In Bulgaria, one of the biggest minority groups is the Gypsies. The Turkish national minority has its political background in Bulgaria. They have their own political party, which has almost ten percent of the seats in Parliament and supports the government. In Bulgaria there are several political organizations of the Gypsies as well. Two of them, the Gypsy Alliance of Bulgaria and the Confederation of Gypsies in Bulgaria are quite important. They have an advisory council with five members which consults the government on matters concerning the Gypsy community. Thy Gypsies - just as in all the other countries in East-Central Europe - live in appalling poverty in Bulgaria. Unemployment rates are very high all over the country, but the Gypsies are exceptionally hard-hit by it to a large extent because of the low level of their education.

As far as cultural autonomy is concerned, the Bulgarian government does not take it very seriously and does not do too much in this respect.

International Agreements
Rinaldo Locatelli

I have to tell you, basically I am not a theorist and an expert in the general fields of international law, but rather a kind of executive as a managing secretary of a committee might be, dealing with the matters of local and regional governments, and as such, my special field is autonomy, which we have heard so much about here at this conference.

The Council of Europe has already had a European Charter on local autonomies. This agreement was adopted and signed by Hungary and other four nations in 1985, and - even more important - it has been ratified by seventeen European nations since then. According to the agreement "local autonomy means the right and the actual possibilities for a local community to take responsibility and manage and control most of the public issues within a certain legal framework at a local level, pursuing the interests of the local population".

Act 4 of the same Charter makes another important statement, which is very topical all over Europe again, namely the principle of subsidiarity. The Charter says the following about it: "As a rule, matters of public interests must be decided on at a level of administration most available to the citizens", which means first at local, then regional, and finally at state and European level. The Charter goes on saying that "devolution of these tasks to other administrative authorities fully depends on the nature of the issue and might be possible for economic and other reasons of efficiency."

There are tasks, of course, that cannot be solved at local level. There is a third part of the charter that may be important for us. It speaks about the defence of the community's territorial borders. Act 5 imposes on local authorities - and mutatis mutandis it applies to regional authorities as well - that in the case of any wish to change the borders they should consult in advance the local communities involved and they can decide on the matter only with the consent of the local community (as a result of a referendum, if the law makes it possible, for example). These questions are of vital importance, but minorities might be more interested in the problems of what we call in Strasbourg "regionalism" or regional autonomy, because their problems are usually raised at that level.

There was a conference in 1978, with a lot of participants representing different regions of Western Europe where we tried to give a definition of regional autonomy. When we speak about regional autonomy we always mean decentralization and devolution of central state authorities but within the framework of the status quo. The 1978 Declaration of Bordeaux, prescribed regional autonomy in the field of culture - and, what was especially important for each minority community, in the field of education. The Declaration demanded proper laws, fixed regulations and general standards concerning education, research and culture. It also demanded that regions should be vested with the right to make cultural agreements directly with other European regions and gave voice to a wish to establish regional medias. It emphasized the importance of the variety of cultures and languages and claimed for equal rights to all regional minorities. Regional autonomy is the best means to accept and assert the great variety of cultures, ethnicities and languages. After 1978, we tried to work in the spirit of the Declaration and based on the results of this conference we organized another one in 1984, this time on the problems of minority languages and invited the representative of both the regions and the minorities. It was at this conference in

Strasbourg that the thought of a Charter concerning regional minority languages was conceived. It was the duty of our committee to prepare the Charter with the help of an elected consultative body and some independent experts. Later, when the proposal got some support from the Parliament, which was very important from a political point of view, after some reservations the Board of Ministers adopted the text and appointed a government committee to examine the proposal. Finally, a couple of years later the Charter was adopted in June 1992, and was signed in November 1992. The Charter asserted specifically cultural aims. Its main object was to support the development and assure the defence of regional minority languages, especially of those in danger and which organically belong to a coherent system of European cultural values. I think especially of languages that are separated. The Charter gives clear instructions regarding these languages considering it illegal to discriminate against them. But it goes much farther and urges the governments to give active and efficient help to support these languages and their speakers and demands that regional minority languages should be used in education as far as possible - there is a whole chapter about this problem - in the media, in administration and justice, especially at local levels, as well as in the fields of economic, cultural and social life. The authors of the Charter, and basically also the governments that signed it, all agreed that these languages - at least in some cases - had to be compensated somehow for the discrimination imposed on them in the past, so they wanted to make efforts and give active help to these languages to survive or revive. The Charter's main concern was to preserve these cultures and languages, but it was also worried about the speakers' circumstances and tried to make all the important aspects of their life easier. At the same time, the principles incorporated in the Charter cannot be reckoned legally of course. Nevertheless, it is a kind of obligation for the signers to provide regional minority languages the status declared in the Charter and make laws supporting this process.

It is important to see that the principles of the agreement were worked out before the crucial changes in East-Central Europe, so the new realities and the newly sprung claims and demands of these countries could not be taken into account in these proposals. But by the time the agreement got in front of the Board of Ministers, some of the representatives of these new regimes - for example the representative of Hungary, among others - had been adopted by this board and took a very active part in working out the final version of the principles. Nevertheless, I have to admit that this agreement does not deal with the defence of the national minorities whose natural right would be to fight for a kind of autonomy and it does not concern itself with the problem of borders either. The only thing it can do is to alleviate the tensions within the framework of the status quo, it cannot claim to be more than a basis for new agreements. The proposal makes it possible for governments to give voice to some of their reservations in connection with certain acts. Hungary has already signed the agreement and Romania has just been adopted as a member of the Council of Europe and is bound to consult the text and the principles of the agreement. Although, the principles laid down in the agreement cannot be enforced by law, I still believe it can serve as a useful basis for a dialogue between the government and the minorities and helps to make it clear how much the government can take these principles on board and how far it is ready to go. At present, we have thirteen states that have signed the agreement, and Hungary is the only country from the East-Central European region which has joined. But the ratification of the agreement is still ahead of us; it has not happened anywhere yet.

Let me continue with some plans that might be more interesting for the minorities because they deal with their problems in a more direct way. In 1990, not long after the crucial changes in East-Central Europe, The European Parliament adopted the first and later, in 1993, the second version of its Proposals. It actually suggests that an amendment should be attached to the European Agreement on the Defence of Human Rights, which means that our proposal should be fitted somehow into that set of individual (not collective!) human rights whose defence is clearly laid down in this agreement and whose compliance can be reckoned by the force of law. As early as February 1991, another organization, called the European Committee of Rights for Democracy, which is a consultative committee and has numerous prominent advisors and experts on constitutional matters as members, also made a proposal for a European agreement on the defence of minority rights. The text of this proposal is still on the table of the governments, at least in Strasbourg. This proposal encompasses not only the individual but also the collective rights of minorities, such as the right to exist and be respected and the right to develop and defend their ethnic, religious and linguistic identities - to mention only the most important ones. The proposal declares that every linguistic community has the right to associate with other linguistic communities, any member of a minority religion has the right to teach and pursue his or her religious beliefs either as an individual or as a member of a community, either privately or publicly. The agreement proposal of the so-called Venice Committee, has worked out a very complicated system of control, which in many respects is very similar to the mechanisms worked out by the European Convent of Human Rights, but according to this proposal, complaints would not be handed in as individual complaints but by groups representing the individual's interests.

We also have to mention some resolutions, for example the ones adopted by the Conference of European Local and Regional Self-governments of Europe in March 1992, which dealt with the problems of minority autonomies, nationalism and the possibilities of a Union of Europe. The document states that in the defence of certain ethnic identities the constitution of some states should be amended to give scope to the defence of minority rights so that these rights might be defended by the force of law.

The Committee urges decentralization of powers and demands an extensive devolution of central authorities to regional and local authorities. At the same time it urges the recognition and the defence of local and regional identities and claims for the right of minorities to take an active part in matters of public interest.

On October 8-9, 1993, the Council of Europe held a a summit meeting in Vienna with the participation of the state and government leaders of the member countries. At this meeting minority issues were often on the agenda and stirred much debate. I would like to quote some parts of the Declaration, which was signed by the state and government leaders of the 32 member countries, among others Meciar, Iliescu and the Hungarian Foreign Minister, who signed the Declaration in the name of the Hungarian Prime Minister, Mr. Antall, who could not take part in the meeting because of his illness. The participating heads of state and Prime Ministers signed an agreement in which they took legal and political responsibility for the observation of minority rights in different

European countries, and they commissioned the Board of Ministers of the Council of Europe to work out the appropriate legal means.

Amendment 2 of the Declaration deals with the minority issue. There are several statements in the Declaration which strongly emphasize the fact that without assuring and defending minority rights in the region we can hardly live in peace and stability in the long run. There are two other principles that can never be violated according to the Declaration, namely those of the constitutional state and territorial integrity. These principles are self-explanatory, or at least they should be. The Declaration also demands that all minority groups should have the right to use their own language and pursue their own cultural traditions and religious beliefs. The Amendment emphasizes the importance of bilateral meetings and agreements, as well as the defence of minority rights and the preservation and maintenance of peace and stability in the region. All the European political leaders agreed that the Council of Europe should do the best in its power to translate these political responsibilities into political obligations that can be guaranteed by the force of law.

All the agreements mentioned above have dealt with local or regional autonomies, which remain within the framework of the status quo and never had any mention about separatism or secession. It is quite evident as well, that autonomy is not a general term in itself, and it always means a concrete form of autonomy.

Let's start with an agreement already in force, namely the Charter of Regional and Minority Languages. It this case it is quite clear that we are speaking about territorial languages, that is languages whose use can be exactly defined geographically. That is why the agreement is about "territories" where these regional or minority languages are used, by which it means not only the territory where these languages are in a dominant or majority position, but also territories where for different historical reasons these languages have become minority languages, sometimes even in regions where they used to be in a central and dominant position. The fact that the most part of the agreement deals with these territorial languages shows it very clearly that the application of these minority rights and principles really needs geographical considerations and on the side of the government. For example, when you are talking about the use of a language within a certain local or regional community, it is quite evident that you do not want to extend it to the whole territory of the country and you have to be exact and define the region where the given community is sufficiently numerous and concentrated (it does not mean it has to be in majority of course) to demand this right. There is act of the Declaration which deals with non-territorial languages, such as the language of the Gypsies or the Jews among others. But it does not concern the essence of the agreement. Naturally, the agreement uses the term "territorial" in a relatively flexible way, since the only thing it ordains is that at the moment of ratification every state is to define exactly which territories it takes upon itself to observe minority rights in. There is another act of the agreement which declares that territories where these regional or minority languages are spoken cannot be discriminated against and all their rights must be respected. According to the agreement it would be desirable to find some correspondence between the language and the administrative units, which would make it much easier to manage and control these territories and their problems. This principle cannot be followed in all cases of course. Sometimes minority communities are extremely scattered and interspersed. But besides language aspects, there

106

are other criteria according to which the administrative division of a country can be made, for example the borders of a settlement, etc. Thus, the agreement does not claim that it is a must that regional or minority language territories and local or regional administrative territories always correspond, but it condemns all administrative measures (for example dividing a language community by attaching them to two different administrative units) that aim at making it more difficult for a minority community to use its native language and assert its own culture and identity. In other words, if in certain cases the administrative-territorial division cannot correspond to the regional-minority language division, it should remain neutral, at least, and should not have a negative impact on the language.

The proposal of the Venice Committee mentioned above is quite exact about this problem. In Act 13 we can read the following: "All states herewith undertake that they restrain themselves from taking or encouraging measures that aim at assimilating different minority communities or changing the ratio of these communities on purpose."

Act 14 says the following: "All states undertake to help and support minority communities to take an active part in public affairs, especially in matters and decisions concerning their own areas."

In Act 11 of the Amendment of the Declaration of the European Parliament, we can read the following: "In regions where certain minority communities are larger in number than the majority community, they are entitled to establish their own local or autonomous administration or obtain a special status according to special local or historical circumstances and in accordance with the national law of the country."

The Council of Europe has an agreement adopted on the status of minority languages; there are two proposals in the pipeline: one of them is a kind of guide-line agreement on minority issues and the other is an effort to fit our principles into that set of individual rights that are laid down in the amendment of the Declaration and are guaranteed by the mechanisms stipulated and controlled by the Human Rights Committee. Besides that, the Council of Europe has been commissioned to give legal and technical help in bilateral agreements between states or regional communities.

Table of Contents